WOMEN LIKE ME

A CELEBRATION OF COURAGE AND TRIUMPHS

JULIE FAIRHURST

ROCK STAR PUBLISHING

Julie Fairhurst – Rock Star Publishing
Paperback Edition ISBN: 978-1-9995503-3-2
Large Print Edition ISBN: 978-1-9995503-4-9

"There is no
greater agony than
bearing an untold
story inside you."

- Maya Angelou -

CONTENTS

INTRODUCTION

Women Like Me – this book could not have a more fitting title. This book was written by women who are just like you, like me, and like all of us. After reading their incredible stories, be sure to go to the author section to read each extraordinary yet everyday woman's biography. You will also say they are Women Like Me.

None of us in this world can escape heartache, insecurities, fear, or feelings of not being good enough. You may not experience them daily, but you will share them at some time in your life. We all will. And when life decides it is your turn, how will you handle what life brings to you?

"Women are like teabags.
We don't know our true strength until we are in hot water."
-Eleanor Roosevelt

Smart lady, Eleanor Roosevelt, and a true statement she spoke. Our real strength shows up at times when life forces us to deal with extraordinary situations. Many of us can relate to situations because maybe you have already been there or know someone who has.

The death of a child. Mental illness. Living in poverty. Addictions. Homelessness. Life altering accidents. Life-threatening illness. Violence. Living in negativity. These are what the women in this book had to face. And face these issues they did.

The ladies in Women Like Me fought their way through their struggles, never giving up, because they knew, in their hearts that there was a light at the end of the tunnel. They decided to choose success over struggle. They kept moving forward even when the future was full of darkness.

I've always said, "it's okay to have a bad day, hide under the covers or fall down, so long as you don't stay there, you must get back up and keep moving forward."

I believe in the power of self-belief. If you believe in yourself, little can stop you from whatever you want to accomplish. It gives you the ability to push forward and defy the odds when things are stacked against you. You will be able to handle life's roadblocks and brush away the naysayers. Self-belief will bring you peace of mind. You will feel stronger while you move forward to achieve your goals.

I believe in gratitude. When you are grateful, even for the small things in your life, that gratitude creates power. What kind of power? The ability to manifest more good things into your life. Gratitude can work magic in our lives. Start to be grateful for the life you have, and the universe will bring you more good things to be thankful for. Try it and watch your life change.

I believe that what comes out of our mouths is a prophecy for our future. If you are putting yourself down, saying negative comments and talking down to yourself, you speak the prediction for your life. What you speak, you will get. Watch your words when you speak to yourself and others.

When you feel that negative self-rant working its way up from your stomach into your throat, ready to jump out of your mouth, stop yourself. Instead, say something kind about you to you. Speak about how you want your life to turn out and how you dream it to be. Keep your self-talk positive, and you will soon see your life begin to turn more positive.

The women whose stories are in this book, Women Like Me, believe in themselves. They are immensely grateful for their lives, the good and the bad. They have learned to speak kindly about themselves; knowing what comes out of their mouths will be their destiny.

They are women like me, women like you, women like us, and they have shared their stories in the belief that it will help others through their struggles. They want to be that shining light in the tunnel for you to follow, so you can find your way through the darkness and emerge into the light so that you can live your best life.

I wish that for you as well.

Julie Fairhurst

QUOTES FROM WOMEN LIKE YOU

I have sprinkled quotes throughout Women Like Me. You'll find encouraging quotes from women who are just like you.

Quotes are essential as they can send you in a different direction rather than where you are heading now by presenting new ideas. They contain wisdom and quite often insight in just a few words, into an easy to read sentence.

Quotes can often give the reader a sense of hope for their life and the situations they are dealing with in their lives. For me, quotes have helped me with inspiration and motivation during my trying times.

It is beautiful to read what other women have written over the years to help other women on their journeys. I appreciate these women, those who went before us, those from who we can learn lessons of love, strength, family, and caring for ourselves.

They are and were Women Like Me.

HAIKU

I also sprinkled Haiku throughout Women Like Me. They are poems in the form of Haiku.

Haiku is a short-form type of poetry originally from Japan. Haiku poetry traditionally discusses abstract subjects or those from the natural world, including seasons, months, animals, and even the smallest elements of nature, down to a blade of grass or a drop of dew. Haiku does not have to rhyme; usually, it does not rhyme at all. It can include the repetition of words or sounds.

Susan Harrison kindly provided Women Like Me with Haiku poems. Susan describes her Haiku writings as this…

Haiku
A tiny window into a scene much larger, spoken in a single breath.
Traditionally a three line poem consisting of the first line having five syllables
The second line is seven syllables and third line is five syllables.
The focus is on nature, the senses, a moment in time.
Red and yellow are the colours of hunger and red alone is the colour of passion.

To be spoken softly, barely a whisper.

I know you will enjoy reading Susan's Haiku poems written with love in Women Like Me.

Rushing Crashing Flash
Impending danger rushing in
Scavenged to the ground.

-Susan Harrison

1

IS THIS AS GOOD AS IT GETS?

HOW I FOUGHT MY WAY OUT OF HOMELESSNESS

Have you ever thought to yourself, "is this as good as it gets?"

It's not like things were super bad. It was like I could see into my future, though, and had started to feel like I could do better for myself and my kids. We weren't too badly off; we were lucky that we'd managed to secure a place to live in a subsidized housing community. I had a little hair salon, set up in my basement, which allowed me to work from home without having to put my two toddlers into daycare. It worked for us – but it wasn't exactly an ideal long-term living arrangement.

Our neighborhood was a rough one. There were a lot of gangs – not the best kinds of people to live around, in other words. It was also a poor neighborhood. But, again, I felt lucky and happy to be able to afford a home on my low income.

After a few years, my teenage son – who had, by this time, unfortunately started to hang around others who were not the best influence – started to get into trouble. At around the same time, the father of my two little ones had begun to exhibit signs of excessive drinking. His behavior was becoming extremely weird. I was starting to get terribly upset as a result of everything that was happening around me. I started to feel trapped in my own life, with no hope of escape. I was falling into a deep depression: a black hole that I could not see any way out of.

One day, I decided to have a conversation about my struggles with my mother who lived on Vancouver Island, in British Columbia. I didn't know how to fix things – but I did know that I needed help.

My mom suggested that I should consider moving out of the Lower Mainland. She said that things would be better if we were to move closer to them.

My parents have always been a great help – but it has also involved a five-hour trip and, therefore, quite an expense to be able to see them. Having given it a great deal of thought, I made the decision to move to Vancouver Island as my mom had suggested.

I knew that we needed to restart our lives. I was scared to leave the security of my subsidized rent. I was really scared to be leaving all my clients as well: my only source of income. But I knew that relocating was a smart move that needed to happen.

Then, the work started! Relocating was terribly hard work; I had to have a plan of action. It wasn't just me; it was me and my three kids! What would be the best way to find a rental home in the new area when we lived so far away? I was also all too aware that moving would require a lot of money. As such, I had to undertake a lot of planning in order to make it happen – but something told me that I was doing the right thing, even if it was going to be hard.

My parents helped by acting on my behalf. I would see homes advertised, make appointments for viewings, and then my dad would go and check out the places for us. I trusted his judgement. I was so grateful when, having viewed a few homes, he was able to secure one for us. It was such a cute place; it was clean and quiet. A completely different community from the one that we were moving from. It felt amazing that we would be able to start all over again.

In making the move, we not only had to leave all of our friends, extended family, and clients behind – but most of our belongings, too. I just couldn't afford a big moving truck. I had a friend that had a small cube truck and we just had to make it work with the room that we had. So, we made the move, and I fell in love with our new home and our new life.

I was a bit lonely at first – but the house was so nice and so was the location. We could walk to the woods in just a few minutes, and we could get to the river or to the beach within a five-minute drive. We had a great summer.

Fall came and I knew that I had to start to integrate my family into the community. My eldest son was able to enroll at a great middle school and my five-year-old son started kindergarten. I needed to find daycare for my four-year-old daughter. And – I needed to find a job. Again: it was hard, but I just felt like I was doing the right thing. We were on our way to bigger and better things.

Then, it happened! I landed a great job in a nice salon; I just loved it. My kids were settling in well, life was looking up for us, and I was feeling happy and positive.

But, then, it all came crashing down. My landlord gave us some bad news. He had to sell the house; he had gone into foreclosure. We were given two months notice to move out. I was devastated.

I had to try to find another home for us as quickly as possible. I knew, as a result of our first attempt – seven months earlier – that it would be difficult. Fortunately, I did manage to find us a new home. It was, in fact, in an even better location; it was right across the street from my eldest child's middle school and, just behind that, the elementary school.

I just loved our new neighborhood. The home was a bit pricey, but I managed it and we were happy. Island life was good. I started to make good connections for the kids and built up a new network of clientele at work.

But then, once again, it all came crashing down. I found a notice on our front door. The landlord was selling the house! Our home was being taken from us once more. I felt defeated; after all our hard work, we were having to move again. I called my mom; I felt so frustrated. The security and the stability that I craved so desperately for myself and my children had been snatched from us; it was all out of my control. What were we going to do? I was growing so tired of all of this and began to feel depressed.

I knew that I couldn't give up. I called my mom; I was trying to figure out potential ways in which I could save up some money so that we could find a home of our own to buy. It seemed like a great idea but, as a single mom of three kids, the dream of being able to afford a mortgage and the down payment that I would need – as well as having money to live on day-to-day seemed to be unachievable.

The cost of a single-family home was so expensive that my only hope was to maybe be able to buy an older apartment or town-house. It was scary because, the longer that it took me to save, the higher the prices would get. Our province was experiencing a housing boom and, every time I watched the news, I would end up feeling defeated. "How will I ever be able to achieve this dream for me and my kids?", I wondered.

I didn't want to keep moving. All I wanted was to be able to have a stable life for my kids' sake as well as my own. So, I came up with a plan. If I didn't pay any rent for 12 to 18 months, I'd be able to save up every spare dollar and would eventually have enough for a small down payment for a home of our own. The only way this plan would work was with the help of my parents. I needed free rent.

I asked my family if we could have a talk; I had a good game plan, but I couldn't do it alone. I needed to see if we could work it out. So, one evening I sat my mom, dad, and aunt down, and explained my rough action plan to them. I needed to know if it were even possible that they could help me.

My mom and dad, and my aunt – who's my mom's best friend – bought their house together. It is a wonderful little rancher with three bedrooms, just 35 minutes out of town. It is a great house – not too large, with a fabulous yard for their three dogs. I knew this was not going to be an easy route to follow for anyone involved; it wouldn't be an ideal situation for any of us. If they agreed, it would be crowded.

But, luckily for me, they said "yes" to my plan! I was so grateful that they were all willing to adjust their lives in order to help me realize my dream of owning a home. How lucky was I to have their support?

It was clear, though, that not all of us were going to be able to fit into this little rancher home; there was just no way. It would simply be way too tight. The alternative would be for me to move into the old RV that they had parked in the yard – and that had not been used for several years.

I thought that this would be doable; I could clean it up and then everything might work out okay. I'd use it as my bedroom and living space. That way, my two younger children would be able to stay inside the house with my teenage son; they could all share the master bedroom.

Back and forth we went, trying to figure out how we'd arrange the rooms. I felt so thankful that my mom and dad had been so selfless in trying to make sure that everything worked out. They were moving their bedrooms around to accommodate us; it really helped me to feel loved and supported. I knew that I was making the right decision; we were ready to make the move.

Once again, I had to downsize; it was a challenge to try to fit all our belongings into my parents' small home. I knew that, if we were to pay for storage space – for the older furniture that I owned – then, by the end of that storage period, the costs just wouldn't amount to good financial sense. So, I got rid of everything! All of our books, kitchen stuff, furniture – everything that wasn't essential to everyday living. It was a very tough thing for me to do. Having downsized just two years ago when I'd moved my little family to Vancouver Island, though, I knew deep down that it was just stuff; we can always get stuff – and we could always get more stuff in the future if we wanted to.

The month that we were about to move into my parents' house, my older son's father suggested that our son should move in with him; they'd never lived together. His dad had a nice home and a new baby on the way; he wanted to have a chance to be a real father to our son before he became an adult. Our son was 17 years old and had one more year left of high school. I was fearful at the idea of not having him close to me, or to his little brother and sister – but the timing seemed perfect, so I agreed. As a result, we didn't have to rearrange all of the bedrooms; we now only had two little ones to worry about.

My dad agreed to move into the smaller guest room so that my 6 and 7-year-old children could share the master bedroom with my mother. We found a set of bunk beds for sale, bought them, and found that there was, thankfully, just enough room for the beds in her room. Dad painted the inside of the old RV for me and, equipped with some fans to help me sleep, I was able to make it work.

I had no bathroom or water – but I did run a power cord from the house to the RV so that I could either plug in a heater for warmth or the fan for cool air. It was all going to work out!

Now, it was the first of December; I'd moved into the RV and the two little ones had moved into the house. Our Christmas was super nice; we had all learned to coexist harmoniously. It was such an amazing time while also being an incredibly hard time for all of us. Living as a cooperative family unit has its challenges as well as its advantages.

Watching my kids thrive in the midst of so much love and attention was such a beautiful experience. I went from being a single mom to almost co-parenting with my parents who were, likewise, there to guide, teach, and love my kids.

The months went by and I stuck to my plan. I was working a lot, carefully saving every penny that I made. I was learning what I needed to do or to improve to be able to obtain a mortgage. I paid off my student loan of $18,000; the day on which I did so, I felt so happy and proud of all the hard work that I'd put in. I was gradually building up my credit – and I continued to save, and save, and save.

I started to make excellent progress. I found that, over time, I was better able to focus and it became easier to stay the course. I wanted a home so badly for my kids – and for me – that the dream occupied almost all my thoughts.

I started to actively investigate property listings. It was difficult; it seemed that house prices were climbing just as fast as I could save. My dream was starting to look unaffordable; I was scared. I'd have to make way more money over the course of a year and I just didn't know how that would be possible. I'd been a hairstylist for over 15 years and was able to support my family – but what it would take to be able to buy our future home was looking to be so much more that I could bring in.

I just kept on saving and looking at the cheapest places available. I was trying to imagine how we'd be able to make it work – at places like a one-bedroom apartment, for instance – and thought to myself "I could sleep on the couch; I could build up some equity and maybe sell it in a couple of years and be able to afford a two-bedroom place. And then, hopefully, I could keep moving up to a bigger and better home."

Then, one day at work, something happened that changed everything. I met a new client and, as I was chatting with her about my life – and her life – we got to know each other while I was working on her hair. I told her about my plan to have my own home one day. I told her how we were living with my parents and my aunt in the little rancher – and I told her about my living quarters in the RV. I explained that I was saving money, emphasizing just how hard I was trying to make sure that we could buy our own home.

She quietly listened to me talking away and then asked, “have you ever heard of Habitat for Humanity?” – to which I responded, “well of course I have”. She explained that she was on the Board of Directors and that they had a lot of plans and projects underway at that time. She told me that I should apply to be a partner family. I said, “oh, yeah”; I didn’t really think that it was an option for me and just sort of brushed it off. I told her that I’d have a look at the website and check it out. As she was leaving, she turned to me and said: “they are looking for families just like you”.

I didn’t think much of it as I’d previously lived in a subsidized housing community with very low rent. I was consequently very wary of low-income community housing projects as my experiences of living there had not been positive ones. I also carried some feelings of guilt about having given up that opportunity, that resource, simply because it did not “fit” my lifestyle anymore.

By the time that I was driving home that night – to my parents’ home – I’d forgotten all about my conversation with my new client. As I walked through the door of the house, my aunt came up to me, super excited, and handed me a flyer. She told me that a man had come into her store that afternoon and had given her the flyer.

Holding the flyer in my hand, I began to read it… “Habitat for Humanity”! And, as I read it, I saw that they were indeed looking for new partner families to become new homeowners in Campbell River. They were going to be hosting an information session at the Campbell River Community Center in just three weeks.

I was in shock! Something inside me just froze. What were the odds of that conversation happening and this flyer appearing in a single day? How had two different people given us the same information? "It must be a sign", I thought.

I told my family about my new client and what she'd told me. We reflected on how remarkable that – the very same day – my aunt had been handed the flyer as well. It felt like it was meant to be.

I asked mom if she'd be willing to go with me to the information night and she agreed. The next week, I printed off the application and filled it out. I thought, "well, why not? I deserve to have the chance to become a homeowner – why not me?". To be accepted would give us opportunities beyond my wildest dreams. What the program offered was so much more than I could ever do on my own. If we were accepted, the home that we'd get would be brand new and big enough for all of us. I felt determined.

I got my application and – oh my goodness: it was intense. I had to provide so much information about myself: my debts, my financial records, my goals, my family and my friends. I needed to submit references with my application, too; it was an incredible amount of work.

I still remember going to the information session with my mom; I was so excited that I hadn't slept the night before. When we left the session that evening, I was super excited about the housing opportunity and the possibility of maybe being accepted.

Now, it was a waiting game; I tried to stay positive. The anticipation was overwhelming! I also had to accept the fact that, even if I were to be accepted as a Habitat for Humanity homeowner, it would involve another year of living with my parents and another cold winter of sleeping in the RV.

I was really having a hard time, trying my best to stay patient and positive. I tried to keep my mind busy, imagining that all of this would eventually work out for the best. I missed being able to sleep under the same roof as my kids. They had a few sick nights – ones that I didn't even know about until the next morning. Over time, I missed them more and more – even though I knew that my family was looking after them.

Time went on. Over the next few months, we all stayed the course, working and saving – and just trying to get along with one another! Then, one day, I got a call from Habitat for Humanity to say that they were looking at my application. How excited we all were! They needed to gather more information from me and said that they would get back to me.

Several weeks went by before they contacted me again. This time, they called me, in order to set up a time at which they could "meet the family": an interview to see if we were good candidates. They were going to come to the little rancher to check out how we were all living.

They had three main criteria. Number one: we had to be in need. Number two: I needed to be able to afford the home and the financial costs that would be attached to homeownership. Number three: I needed to be able to undertake the 500 hours of work required; this work was like a down payment, only it wasn't money – it was my time and labor.

A few weeks later, a few wonderful women came to the house. They were family selection volunteers; they asked us all a lot of questions and met the family dogs. I was able to show them my little RV bedroom and my mom's shared bedroom with my kids. Our sacrifice was all too apparent; we were trying so hard to make a decent life for ourselves so that we could all grow happily and healthily – and be comfortable. When they left, I reflected on the visit; I felt good about it.

So, again, weeks went by, and I hadn't heard anything from them. It was an incredibly stressful time! Eventually, they called and told me that they needed to make another visit to us – this time with the Head of Family Services and the Executive Director. Oh, my goodness: this was getting real.

Again, the interview seemed to go really well, and I felt good about it. Then, I was left to wait. It seemed that there was a lot of waiting involved in those long months.

One day, while I was working, I heard my cellphone ring. When I had a chance to check my messages, I saw that there was one from Habitat for Humanity, asking me to stop by – maybe on my lunch break? – the next day. I was super worried and excited in equal measure. I didn't even manage to sleep that night. Was it going to be good or bad news? I was freaking out.

The next day – during my 40-minute lunch break – I made my way over to Habitat Restore. They led me into a boardroom in the back where there were about half a dozen people sitting at a large table.

One of these people was the woman from our first interview: the family selection volunteer. She had a huge smile on her face. My heart was racing; it felt like it was going to jump right out of my chest. As I sat down, the woman said: "we would like you and your family to partner with us to be a homeowner".

I couldn't contain my emotions; I started crying. I thanked everyone; they were all so nice. Tears were streaming down my face. It was an incredible moment for me.

They asked me to sign a few pieces of paper: the contract. The contract stated that I was on board and that I needed to complete 500 hours of Habitat for Humanity work. After signing it, I returned to work. It had been an amazing 40 minutes of my life.

I wanted to tell the kids as soon as possible. They had been through all of this with me – every step of the way. It had been hard on them as well. After work, I picked up two shiny helium balloons that had "you did it" written across them. I went to their school to pick them up.

As I walked across the field to them, they became extremely excited at seeing the balloons; they asked, "what did we do"? I explained that we had managed to get the house. They both started to scream and jumped up and down. It was just so amazing to see that they were just as happy as I was.

On our way home from school, I explained that – because our home hadn't yet been built – we'd need to stay at Gramma's, Grandpa's, and Auntie's little house for a little while longer. I also wanted them to know that I was going to be terribly busy with my full-time job on top of having to get my 500 hours of work done for Habitat. It was part of the deal: that I help to build my home and my neighbors' homes. So, I told the little ones that they would need to be patient – but that, in the end, it would all be worth it.

Five months later, we did it! We were able to start our new lives in our brand-new home. We finally got our keys on December 13th.

There was even a key ceremony. I was so proud of myself, my kids, and my family; it was incredibly hard work for all of us. But it was all so, so worth it.

We spent Christmas in our new home. It was an amazing Christmas gift: the gift of our forever home.

Samantha Syvret

"I know God will
not give me anything
I can't handle.
I just wish he didn't
trust me so much."

- Mother Teresa -

2

FACING MORTALITY

MY NEW APPRECIATION OF LIFE

Life is all about change. It never stays the same for very long; something new is always around the corner. I am a firm believer that life is what you make it and that a positive mindset beats out the negative every time – but I didn't always feel this way. I will now try, in my own way, to tell you how my life perspective has changed over the last year. My story begins in January 2019.

I moved back home. I had been away for fifteen years in beautiful British Columbia. and it was time to return to my hometown; St. Catharines, Ontario. I was 62 years old and starting another brand new chapter of my life. I moved in with an old friend for a "roomie" and life seemed new and exciting again, a little scary, but still exciting. It was fun to reconnect with my old friends and to rediscover the city that I'd been raised in. Things had changed over the years.

One night, in late June, I woke in the middle of the night and had to go to the bathroom. I didn't feel too well and I thought I had the dreaded "runs" until I looked at the toilet paper and saw that what had been running out of me was actually blood.

The next morning I was up at the crack of dawn and waiting for the clinic to open. The doctor who saw me gave me a rectal exam and then told me he was going to set me up with a specialist. He didn't make a big deal out of it. He told me that we would get my little problem taken care of. I felt relieved.

July was a busy month. Not only did I have a colonoscopy, CatScan, MRI scan and blood tests, I had been forced to find an apartment that I could afford on my own; my roommate and I were just not getting along. Moving is hectic and I really had no time whatsoever to worry about my health. Most of my friends who knew about my predicament told me not to worry, they said that it was probably just hemorrhoids. I tended to believe them. I wanted to believe them.

July 31st: time to go to the surgeon for my test results. Was I scared? Hell yeah. I brought one of my close friends to the appointment with me; I figured that she would be able to remember everything the doctor had to say if I couldn't. It was a good thing I brought her with me. The tumor in my rectum was very low down. The doctor did not think that any surgeon could save my rectum. I would need to have a colostomy bag for the rest of my life. What?!?! And then...

The doctor told me that they had found something else. I truly don't remember if it was found in the CatScan or the MRI scan or both. There was a growth on my heart.

WHAT!?! There was a cardiologist's office next to my doctor and they were friends. Before I knew it, I was in the cardiologist's office and had some kind of test performed. Then, the cardiologist set me up for a few more tests. I think that I was in shock; nothing was really sinking in. This was one heck of a day.

While I was finding out about all of these things, I didn't feel sick. I would get dizzy sometimes if I stood up too fast – but I just put that down to having high blood pressure. I also had a few issues with bowel control but, again, just attributed these issues to my age and my diet. It was only the bleeding that really alerted to me to the fact that something was wrong. How could I feel so good and yet be so sick?

I was told that I'd have to have heart surgery. I could die. If I didn't have heart surgery I definitely would die. I think it is easier to be strong when there are no decisions to be made – when you have no choice. You just have to do what you have to do and hope for the best. I have to say that, when I think back on my journey, a lot of it was surreal; it was like living in a dream.

The tumor on my heart was attached by means of a thin thread. The main concern was that it would break away and, in doing so, create a blockage. They would never have known about my heart problem if I hadn't had cancer. In some respect, you could say that cancer saved my life.

You always hear folks complaining about the health system and how long it takes to get anything done. You hear them saying how they have to wait for months and months just for a test – never mind surgery. Everything happened so quickly for me that it scared me. Was I in so much danger that it all had to be done as soon as possible?

I found out about my heart problem and my "poop bag" for life all in one day. Twenty-six days later, on August 26th, I was having open-heart surgery at Hamilton General Hospital.

The surgery went well. I was pretty out of it for a couple of days. By the fourth day, I was a grumpy cat who had seriously had enough. I never thought of it at the time but it was my fourth day without being able to have a cigarette. It was probably the reason why I freaked out and pretty much checked myself out of the hospital.

I spent the next two weeks at Chez Jeffaine; a lovely spot where the food is good, the atmosphere calm and the company superb. I can never thank my friends enough for allowing me to stay in their home and for taking great care of me during my recovery.

Six weeks and two days after that on, October 9, 2019, I had colon cancer surgery at St. Catharine's General Hospital. There they removed both the tumor and my rectum and gave me a stoma: an asshole coming out of my stomach. It was the day my life truly changed forever.

I thought having my breastbone cracked open and surgery on my heart was going to be the harder operation of the two. I was very wrong. The heart surgery seemed like a breeze compared to colon cancer surgery.

I'd been sliced up the front, sliced up the back.... well, let's just say that I was sliced and diced and then put back together.

Did you know that you still fart even when you don't have a rectum? Yup. I found that out in the first few days of having my stoma. It even sounds like a regular bum fart. Really! I thought my story could use a little comic relief.

My recovery from the second surgery was longer – and much more painful – than the first. After two weeks, having popped my butt stitches, I had to have them resewn. They basically sewed my butt cheeks together, I've gotta say, though, I still look good in a pair of jeans.

Nurses visited me at home a few times a week in order to check on me for the first month and a half. After that, their appearances slowly dwindled until I was deemed to be capable of taking care of my stoma by myself. I remember being terrified that I'd have no one to help me. In no time at all, though, I was changing my bag like a pro.

I am slowly adjusting to living with a stoma. There are times when I stink up the bathroom, times when I fart at inappropriate moments because I have no bodily control in that capacity, and times when I have to deal with the ignorance of people who haven't taken the time to understand what having a "poop bag for life" entails.

It has been harder emotionally than it has physically. I am different, now, from other people. I can never change that. I must accept things as they are, and I have.

The cancer was caught at stage one. As a result, I did not have to have chemotherapy. I was lucky that it was caught so early.

I am alive.

Now, I must tell you that I have suffered from depression throughout my life. I think that I have spent more time crying than laughing, more time worrying than enjoying myself. It took two major rounds of surgery to make me realize just how much time I have wasted as well as how little time there really is for each of us.

After months of recovering, I decided that a trip back to British Columbia to see my daughter and grandchildren was in order. I had been housebound for months, after all. This was in February 2020. I left on February 19th and returned March 5th… and then came COVID19. By March 15th everyone was in lockdown. I am glad that I was able to spend two weeks with family before having to spend even more time in isolation.

I am living alone for the first time in years, have health issues up the yin-yang, I am scared and I am lonely… But, guess what? I'm okay. I'm actually really good. I enjoy so many small things now: taking time for myself, actually doing and enjoying the hobbies that I've put off for so long, spending time whenever possible with friends and family, making those extra phone calls just to talk to someone and also to make sure they are doing okay.

I also find myself enjoying the sky view – whether sunny or cloudy, it is all amazing. They are all little things I just took for granted before. I refuse to cry anymore about things over which I have no control. I choose to be happy. I wish that I had realized earlier on in my life that happiness is a choice. I have wasted many years.

When you look your mortality in the face your whole perspective on life changes.

Now, I try to look at everything from a positive point of view. When I feel myself starting to fall into the darkness of depression, I start to think about all the things I have to be grateful for. I am blessed with good family and friends. I am here. Sure, things are different – but I am here.

I am not sure what the moral of my story is – I just know that it felt good to get it down on paper. Thanks for listening.

My final thought…

The day we are born is the beginning of the end. Live every day to it's fullest.

Christine Luciani

"I am no bird; and no net ensnares me: I am a free human being with an independent will."

- Charlotte Bronte -
(Jane Eyre)

3

BECOMING OF LOVE

GRATEFUL FOR EVERYTHING THAT LED ME HERE

At the age of 19, I never thought I'd be living a life of such complications, stemming from the situations I had experienced up until this point in my life. When I was little, people would ask me what I wanted to be when I grew up – and I always gave them the same answer: a wife and a mother. And I achieved both roles – several times.

Daniel

My first marriage was to an older man who had formerly been my neighbour. I had known Daniel for years. I was drawn to him because he was familiar to me; I'd known him for some time. He came from a good family, had a good job, and had a stable lifestyle. He seemed like, and was such a nice person.

After a few months of dating Daniel, I became pregnant with my first child. Daniel proposed and I accepted. Thus, my first marriage began.

I had never been shown what a healthy relationship should look like. I was, as such, walking into this marriage blind. I only knew what I saw and imagined would be good – and I wanted to pick something that was not bad. So, I married him, and we started our journey together.

I craved to have a sense of roots – of belonging somewhere. I was young and, although Daniel was a nice person, being with him intensified my feelings of rejection.

I always think back to our wedding and how uninvolved I was in it all. I was embarrassed by all of the attention that was being shown to me – so much so that I did not participate in our wedding in any way other then saying "Yes" during the ceremony itself.

My experience of being in this relationship was characterized by one main feeling: I always felt that he had "settled" for me. We bought a house together – but I don't remember picking it out. I'm not sure that we even made it to our first anniversary.

Our son was just 5 months old when we parted ways. When I told him that I wasn't happy, he didn't seem too upset. To me, that just confirmed that I'd never been good enough for him. That's what my mind told me, anyway.

We have always remained friends.

Charbel

Immediately after I'd separated from Daniel, I once again sought something – someone – familiar. I started to see a man with whom I'd previously had a relationship, prior to my marriage to Daniel.

Charbel led me to believe he was going to protect me and care for me. He made me feel that I had nothing to worry about. It was all good. Three months later, I moved in with him; a month after that, I found myself pregnant with my second child.

Charbel seemed like the perfect husband. He had a family whom he loved and with whom he seemed close. He owned a home and already had a son – whom he adored. It felt right.

I imagined myself to feel incredibly loved by him. I never felt like he'd "settled" for me; I believed that he loved me more than anything. However, I discovered, over time, that I'd mistaken his possessiveness and controlling behaviour for love. At some point, the physical and emotional abuse started. This again compounded my feelings of inadequacy; to me, such treatment only served to confirm that I was unworthy.

I realize, now, that part of the reason as to why Charbel made me feel "safe" was because he wanted me and only me – and because he wanted to protect me from the world. But, in terms of "protecting" me – he sought to do so by isolating me. It was all terribly confusing. It made me look hard at myself every day, wondering what part I'd played in it all.

I stayed for 5 years. Charbel's control of and physical abuse toward me got worse and worse over the years. I felt like I was being beaten down – emotionally. It's hard to walk away from control. There's fear – so many emotions around it. I felt like he was going to hunt me down; I knew that he would hunt me down.

I tried to leave so many times. Whenever I did leave, I just ended up returning to him. It seemed easier to do that than to try to deal with him and his obsession with me.

Eventually, I became pregnant with a second child with Charbel – my third child. When that child was 5 days old, I knew that I had to leave.

When I said that I was leaving, Charbel immediately threatened to take my children away from me. I felt so much fear and confusion inside of me; I didn't know what to do, which way to turn. But I knew that I couldn't go back to him; it wasn't safe.

I moved in with a girlfriend of mine, together with my three children, and felt safe at last. Safe, that is, until the day that Charbel found out where we lived. His threats were endless. I was in incredible fear for my life – and I was very worried about my children.

My first husband, Daniel, spoke to me about my situation and his fear for our son: my firstborn. I agreed with Daniel's suggestion and allowed him to take our son to live with him. It was the right thing to do. We needed to keep him safe.

Eventually, Charbel was to take our two children to his home for a visit. I agreed to meet him so that he could take them for the weekend. That ended up being a major mistake on my part: an instance of terrible judgement. As Charbel drove away from me, with our two children in his truck, he yelled out the window: "good luck ever seeing them again!".

Years of hell followed that. He wouldn't let me see the children. When I managed to speak with them on the phone, I could always hear him in the background, yelling abusive things and calling me nasty names. It was hard to have a relationship with my children as a result of Charbel's outrageous behaviour.

Mike

I met my third husband when he called and booked an appointment with me for a haircut. I was immediately drawn to – attracted to – him. He had a quiet presence about him which I found extremely attractive. He was a bodybuilder and I liked working out, too, so we had something in common.

The week that I met Mike, I had just given custody to my ex-husband. I had signed my two boys over to him, praying that it would stop all of the fighting and terror that Charbel was bringing into my life.

Mike had been brought up with a religious background. Just prior to when I met him, he'd been through a nasty divorce and had decided to start going to church again. I really liked that about him: his relationship with God. I had a lot of religious clients and they all seemed to be so happy. I knew that this relationship would be good for me; Mike and I would be happy, too.

Mike didn't drink or smoke – he was enthusiastic about all things health related. Again, I really liked that about him. Mike was so different from the other men who I'd had in my life. He was like a breath of fresh air. I felt like he'd protect me and care for me – something that I craved so desperately.

Within a year, I found myself pregnant again. Five months later, Mike and I got married. I really felt that he was the love of my life. He was the one I'd been searching for – my forever love.

When our baby arrived, it was another little boy for me. He was born on my 27th birthday and that made his birth even more special. After he was born, I decided to have my tubes tied. Mike already had a son. Now that we'd had our own little one, too, we both decided that we didn't want to have any more children.

I was so fertile that I'd even previously gotten pregnant while I'd been on birth control. Having a tubal ligation seemed like a smart move in the right direction.

As much as I loved this new little fellow in our lives, he reminded me of my horrible feelings of loss for my two older boys.

I went to church with Mike and, in the beginning, it filled a part of me that seemed to be missing. However, as time went on, I found myself mad at God and wanted to stop going to church.

I couldn't understand why God would allow my two boys to be pulled away from me to live in an abusive household with their father. He made me angry – and sad.

I couldn't face seeing all of the happy families at church every Sunday. It made me feel like I wanted to hide and that I wasn't good enough in some way. How could I deserve a good and happy life when my boys weren't living happy lives themselves? It was another reminder that my life was a failure. I just couldn't take it.

Mike had a real hard time with my decision to stop going to church. He simply never understood how attending church could cause me such stress and anxiety. It was very conflicting for me, it became such a big issue between us. Given all the stress with the children and control, it added to the destruction of our marriage.

For approximately three years after splitting up with Mike, I remained single - but I became a serial dater. I can't even count how many dates I went on during this time in my life. It was obvious that I was searching for something to fill a void.

As well as all of this, I was still in an ongoing legal custody battle with Charbel. My children were living in such a nasty environment that I was doing everything in my power to secure custody of them.

Barry

During this time, a client of mine introduced Barry to me. Once again, I thought that I'd found my saviour. It was as though my life up until that point had involved, me having run a marathon - but then Barry had stopped his car alongside me and offered me a ride. I got into that car, knowing that it was the wrong decision to make, but I was just so tired that I did it anyway.

It was a whirlwind relationship. Within six weeks, we were in Las Vegas, getting married. "What a stupid mistake", I realized right away. My life in this period was so stressful and challenging that I'd jumped at the first chance for someone to rescue me. I know now that only I can rescue me; I have to rescue myself.

My marriage to Barry was truly short-lived. Once I'd realized my mistake, I quickly ended it.

I eventually won legal custody of both of my boys from Charbel. It was amazing to have all four of my children under my roof full-time, all together at last. I was in heaven; I was so happy. This domestic bliss lasted for several months - until Charbel secured his first visit, unsupervised.

The first time that the boys went for an unsupervised visit with Charbel after I'd regained custody of them, he took them to his home – which was a four-hour drive away. On Sunday, when the boys were due to return home, I received a phone call from one of the boys. My 11-year old son told me that they weren't coming home and that, if I tried to come and collect them, they were going to tell the authorities that I'd abused them.

I immediately jumped in my car and started the four-hour drive to pick them up. But, you know – when you're alone in a car, driving through the mountains, you get a chance to think and to gain some clarity.

I realized that, if I continued this battle with Charbel, there'd be no winners. My other two boys were at home, suffering greatly as a result of all of the turmoil that this toxic situation was causing. I also thought that, if I walked away, my two boys would actually be better off; I was the common denominator and the intended recipient of the brunt of Charbel's anger. I was clearly the problem.

So, I decided to save my two boys at home – and to let Charbel win.

Nicko

And then there came Nicko. Nicko had always been in my life; he'd been my first love in my early teen years. He'd always been around – and we'd managed to sustain a friendship. I knew his family very well and they seemed like a real tight family – as any Greek family would.

Nicko and I never did officially get married – but we lived as a common-law couple for six years. Nicko felt like home. He had been a constant in my life and he knew my children. There was nothing that I needed to explain to him; he was aware of it all.

Nicko didn't have any children and we wanted to have children together. So, two years into our relationship, I had my tubal ligation reversed and along came our beautiful little girls.

I'd always thought that Nicko was a free spirit. However, I realized that he wasn't a free spirit; he was just irresponsible. What I came to learn was that Nicko had been dependent on his family for his whole life. Financially, they'd always been there to help him whenever he'd asked for money. Now, that had become my job: to bankroll him.

Nicko's family was very traditionally Greek. His mom – whom I adored – wouldn't even let Nicko be alone with our daughters. She considered it to be a "woman's job" – as if men were incapable of parenting.

So, not only did I start to bear all of the financial responsibilities for our family, but I also had to undertake all of the parenting as well.

I'd always had great success with my hairdressing business; I'd always done well. So, the money was there – but I had to work incredibly long hours to make it. The long hours that I spent working, together with the exhaustion of full-time parenting, without any help, began to take their toll on me.

Nicko became just another child for whom I needed to care for. He complained continuously about the number of hours I worked – but he offered me no relief.

Finally, I'd had enough. When our second daughter was 6 months old, I found myself a 40-year-old single mother of six.

Wade

A couple of years later, and after a couple of subsequent relationships, I met Wade. He seemed to be a nice guy who'd had a bit of a troubled past. Wade was recognized in the community for helping others. He was someone who people looked up to. On paper, he looked good.

We were married within three months. I felt pressured into this marriage. I thought that I loved him – but the last thing that I wanted to do was to get married again. He, on the other hand, really wanted to marry me. He constantly pressured me by saying, "if you were willing to get married before, why wouldn't you marry me?".

I thought that he would fit into my life, given all the situations and circumstances – but I was somewhat confused and wasn't sure what I should do. I agreed to marry him, thinking it was doing the right thing to do. The next thing I knew, I had another ring on my finger. Wade and I were married.

Well, that was another disaster. Two months later, I had to lock myself in the bathroom when he got drunk and became emotionally abusive. In that state, he'd call me every name in the book – even in front of the children. Again, I found myself and my children in a volatile situation, wondering how did I get here again.

Wade would stop drinking several times over the course of our relationship and, when he did, it was better. However, the back and forth of his drinking and erratic behaviour was too much for me. I couldn't take it any longer. Not only was it affecting me, it was affecting the kids as well. I decided that enough was enough. I ended it.

I moved to the countryside with my two daughters as the boys were older, now, and wanted to live on their own. I decided that it was time to live a simpler life and to focus on my girls and my family.

We loved our little place; it was peaceful. We had nightly campfires. We ate fresh eggs from our chickens. We were content. The girls and I were happy.

One day, a girlfriend of mine came by and we decided to take my two girls out for a bike ride. As we went down a hill, I hit a bit of gravel – and that's the last thing I remember. I wiped out, was thrown down a ditch and was unconscious for ten minutes.

As it turned out, I had a severe brain injury. I'd lost my ability to speak; I couldn't even get out of bed on my own. I had severe vertigo and slept all of the time. I had to be cared for as I couldn't care for myself, let alone my girls.

Sometimes, life gives us what we need in the most unusual way. When this happened, I knew that it was meant to be. I desperately needed to have a rest – time off from life. When you can't talk and you can't really walk, it forces you to take the ultimate vacation.

It was about 3 months before I could go back to work. Even then, I only returned to work part-time. It was exhausting for me – not only because of the physical work but because everyone wanted to know what had happened. I had a difficult time speaking as the head injury had caused me to develop a bad stutter.

Tony

As I was in the process of healing, I met Tony, who became my ultimate hero. He loved me even though I stuttered; he accepted me in spite of my head trauma. He had lived next door to my boys and Charbel while my boys were growing up. He was aware of the history – one of my boys had even worked for him.

Given all of that, once you meet in that context, how can you even think that this is not supposed to be? Tony was a master at saying the right things; he was so good at reassuring me that everything was going to be okay. I believed every word he spoke.

I was put on the highest pedestal that you could ever possibly imagine. Tony accepted me for me – the inside me – not for the way I looked or how much money I made or how I looked on his arm and made him feel. Tony was deep – and his emotions and love for me ran the deepest.

Two years after our romance began, we married in our backyard. I didn't want to get married again. Tony lived four hours away; I could already see signs of control. Tony had three young children – which I knew would be a lot of work. Tony assured me that we'd be in this together and that I had never really had an actual husband. He explained that a real husband looks after his wife and children – and that he was going to do just that. So, reluctantly, I agreed to get married once more.

On the day of our wedding, my two estranged sons were there to give me to Tony, whom they had known their whole lives. They carried me in at our wedding ceremony. I was positive that Tony was the right man for me. I was confident that Tony would look after me because he had already watched over my boys.

Tony moved into my home and our life together began. But so, too, did the stress.

I soon discovered that life with Tony was not as he'd described. Financially, it was a massive burden for me. As it turned out, Tony had put his company in my name because he was not financially responsible. The debts just continued to grow, month after month.

His children were a lot of work; they came with their own set of dynamics. A blended family was difficult. They'd been raised differently from how I'd raised my own children.

I began to realize; Tony was part of the cycle of control. Once again, I had missed all the signs that were there right from the start. He began to set a lot of rules. He made me change my phone number. He didn't want me to have male clients – and he didn't want me to have certain female clients. He wanted to control my friendships as well as my relationships with my older children. It was a kind of control that I'd never experienced before. He went through my phone on a daily basis – which, of course, caused arguments.

Ultimately, Tony didn't want me to have a past – to have had a life before him. I wasn't allowed to speak of any of it. I had to tell my friends not to mention anything about my exes or my past. I couldn't even say the names of my children's fathers in his presence.

During my seven years with Tony, I realized that he was an addict and already had – or had developed (I don't know which) – a mental illness. This made it hard for me to leave him – because I knew the kind, strong, loving person who was inside him. Ultimately, I had no choice but to leave; his behaviour became too bizarre and my girls were afraid.

. . .

Myself

So began the most important relationship that I would ever have in my life. I knew that I could love her. I knew her better than anyone – and so I held her as she grieved.

It was anything but romantic. I was scared – and it was extremely hard and so very lonely. I had never been so alone before.

I cried for the first year. I was not just mourning the loss of my recent relationship – I was grieving for the life that I was never going to have.

I had dreamed of loving somebody so much, having babies with him and building a life together. I had pictured that life so many times. I had to sit down and accept it all: that it simply wasn't to be.

Nothing that I had dreamed of was meant to be. I had to accept my part in it and to understand that I was the common denominator in it all. I had done all of the wrong things for the right reasons. I had married so many times because I'd believed – because I'd been hopeful. I didn't want to see my own self; I didn't want to have to go through the pain.

I had so many children because, again, I wanted to love and to love somebody completely. Ultimately, though, I'd been running from the girl who needed love most of all. I needed to nurture and to be nurtured.

It was mainly my grandson who taught me as I watched him beg to be loved when he first came to live with me. I recognized myself in his behaviour. Watching him grow and feel safe helped me to understand that we can all heal – especially if we feel good inside.

So, together, we began the journey of healing and acceptance. And, the beginning of our new chapter.

WOMEN LIKE ME

Michelle Bisgrove

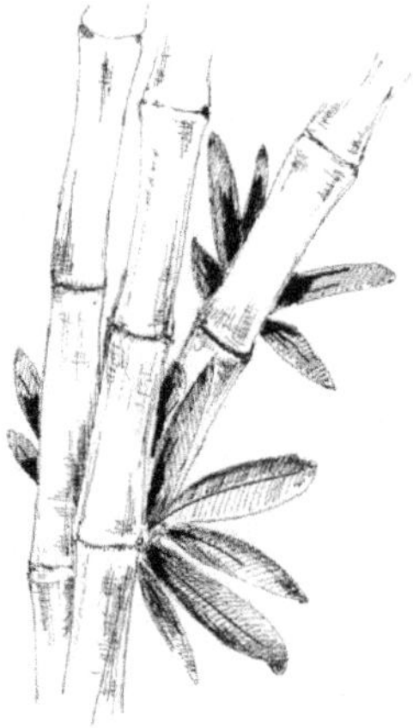

Summer is full, ripe
Mother Nature's arms laden
Bosom in decay?

-Susan Harrison

4

SEEDS OF NEGATIVITY

MOVED ME TO ACTION

I am a highly paid professional. I laugh just typing that – not because I am not a highly-paid professional, but because I was once told that I would never get, or be able to keep, a job.

I come from a family of five: mom, dad, two sisters, and myself. My dad was just a wee bit outnumbered, being the only male in a house full of females. I was the middle child who actually looked like the eldest. I was bigger than my sisters, cousins, and friends. I developed early; I was a young child in a developed teenage body.

In grade three, I became really sick and missed most of the school year as a result. On top of having anemia, I ended up getting the worst case of mononucleosis (or "mono") – now that really is a mouthful. Looking back, now, I think that my suffering from both anemia and mono in the same year laid the foundation for me being perceived as being "lazy"; they're two illnesses that make you feel extremely tired.

We lived in South Burnaby (British Columbia) that year and, at the end of the school year, my parents decided to move to North Burnaby (British Columbia). Since we were moving and I would be attending a new school, they decided to hold me back so that I could repeat grade 3. The new kids wouldn't need to know. Now, though – rather than just being bigger than all of the girls – I also towered over all of the boys. Except for the one who had been held back for 3 years, that is. I digress!

Some of the enduring names that I was given in my new school were "Heather the Happy Hippo" and "Hot Lips". I can't repeat one of them due to it being racist (Black Lives Matter) – and I am not even black. In fact, because I had both anemia and mono, I couldn't have been whiter. One of the symptoms of anemia is pale skin – from a lack of oxygen or blood flow – and the paleness with which mono is associated results from having a low red blood cell count.

In the second year of grade 3, I started my period while wearing a white pair of pants at school – could it get any better than that…? Although I wasn't teased, it was embarrassing. I was younger than most girls when I started – by as much as 3 to 4 years – and I wasn't prepared. Someone had forgotten to have the necessary conversation with me.

Dad was extremely protective of me. While my sisters, cousins, and friends were allowed to walk up to Hastings (Burnaby Heights) to go shopping in their two-piece bathing suits, I wasn't allowed out of our yard wearing anything less than a turtleneck and blue jeans. I remember one day when I was sitting alone on the front porch in my one-piece bathing suit (with circles cut out on each side) and the paperboy was approaching. Dad made me come into the house until the paperboy had gone by.

I recall, too, how mad my mother was when we were getting on the bus and they made her pay the full adult fare for me. That wasn't pretty – she was so mad, like it was my fault.

I have always been okay with me: my own company. I would rather stay at home by myself than go out with the family. I'd sit on the floor, watching TV; I loved TV. In today's world, that would be the same as kids being glued to their devices on social media or gaming. My family could come home and, as long as they didn't walk between me and the TV, I wouldn't even know that they were there.

Growing up, I was tough: a tomboy. My dad taught me how to fight. I remember my dad telling me: once they're down, don't let them back up. He treated me – raised me – like the son he never had. Dad used to go hunting every year, up to the Kootenays: Kimberley, Cranbrook and Nelson. He would ask me if I wanted to go and, of course, I did. It became really clear once we got there, though, that I was just invited as his company for the road trip. He never took me "hunting". While he was out hunting with his friends, I went hunting with his cousin.

Don't get me wrong: I knew that I was a girl, but I used the fact that Daddy raised me like a boy to my advantage – or so I thought. My girlfriends would be in the basement, talking about the boys, and I would be in the driveway getting dirty with the boys (okay, working on cars!). This led me farther down the same path, making me just another "one of the boys" for most of my adolescent life.

Dad and I had a tug-o'-war relationship; he would say "black", I would say "white". He would say "it is going to rain this afternoon" and I would say "no, it is going to be sunny".

I was two months shy of my fourth birthday and sitting 2 feet from the TV screen when President John F. Kennedy was shot right in front of me. The scene has imprinted itself on my brain. I remember how every year, on the anniversary of Kennedy's assassination, my dad and I would debate whether or not Lee Harvey Oswald had killed him. It didn't really matter what I thought, to be honest – what my true opinion was, that is; if Dad said Lee Harvey Oswald had killed Kennedy, I would say that he hadn't. I loved debating with my dad. It wasn't just an argument; I would make a special trip to the library, just to undertake some research. I would recreate the scene three-dimensionally. The Grassy Knoll, the Texas School

Book Depository, the motorcade, the Lincoln limousine...fond memories!

When I reached the end of elementary school and the beginning of high school, I wanted to play soccer – but there were no girls' teams. So, I joined the boys' soccer team in grade 8. Our coach hated it; "girls don't belong on the soccer field", he said. The more he pushed, the more I pushed back. One day, I went out onto the field and sprained my ankle. The coach questioned "if it's so dangerous, why do you insist on playing?" It's because no one tells me that I can't do something. Sometimes I don't think before I speak, though; I replied: "walking across the street is dangerous but you still do it!"

I was playing soccer across the highway from where my dad worked. It had been raining and, at the end of the game, I was covered in mud. I went over to the warehouse to wait for my dad to finish work. Caked in mud, and with my short pixie haircut, all of the truck drivers mistook me for a boy.

My dad tended to use reverse psychology on me. I am not sure why he didn't – to my knowledge – use it on my sisters, though. If he told me that I was lazy, I would get off my ass and get out, looking for work. He would often say that I was lazy; I could never hold down a job. Jobs don't come looking for you.

When I was in grade 11, he said to me "you may as well quit school, you're never going to graduate anyway". I was shocked and dumbfounded by his words. Unbeknown to him, I had already graduated – 6 months earlier. You'd think that I would have wanted to rub it in his face – but I never did tell him. Nah, I was a keep-my-cards-close-to-my-chest type of girl.

I always ended up doing the opposite of what people expected of me. Stubborn. You know the saying: "No one tells me that I can't do something."

I got a job at Denny's, working the graveyard shifts. One night, one of the customers said that he was going to move to Calgary, Alberta. I still shake my head about what I did next – I replied, "not without me!" I went to the manager's office and asked for a transfer. It was Calgary Stampede season; it was a pretty sure bet that I was going to get the transfer. The next day, I went home and told my parents that I was moving.

I moved to Calgary and worked 3 jobs – leaving me with barely enough time to get from one to the other. "Sleep"? – what was that?! No one was going to tell me that I was lazy.

Yes: my dad had created a workaholic. I showed him.

I remember when I lived in a rooming house. The only place in which the single bed could go was under the window. That window had a hole in it, though – and it was the middle of the winter in Calgary. It reminded me of when my parents used to say to me "I walked to school uphill, both ways, bare feet in the snow". My story was a true one, though.

I called my parents, asking if I could borrow some money for food, but the response was "we can't, we just helped your sister buy a car." I never asked for anything again – ever!

Fast forward: I'm 19, working 3 jobs, not exactly in the greatest marriage – and I get pregnant. Yes, I got married and became pregnant in the same year. The doctor has told me that I couldn't get pregnant: surprise! I got through the whole pregnancy; the baby was due on Christmas Day, 1979. The doctor said that, if I hadn't gone into labor by Christmas Day, then he would induce me on Boxing Day. He'd lied for the second time, though.

When I hadn't gone into labor and the doctor hadn't induced me, I asked him if I could drive to British Columbia. He said "No" – but no one tells me that I can't do something. I was constantly being told, "you will be in labor for a long time with your first". In my 19-

year-old brain, though, if I went into labor in between towns, I could just turn back or head onward into the next.

So, more than 9 months pregnant, I made the journey – in the middle of winter – from Alberta to British Columbia. I arrived at my parents' place on New Year's Eve; they weren't home. I could hear that a party was underway at the neighbors' house. I knocked on their door at one minute to midnight, feeling as though I were bigger than a house. Although I myself was "expecting", my arrival itself was unexpected; no, I had not told my family that I was pregnant. The neighbor called my parents to the door; "you are going to want to come and see this", she said to them. My son was born on January 5th, 1980 following 36 hours of labor.

Things had come full circle: I was now living back at my parents' house with a beautiful baby boy. I never did go back to Calgary.

Fast forward four and a half years: my second child was born, a beautiful baby girl. My husband was certainly not a "good" one; he was a deadbeat who had been chased "out of Dodge", as my uncle phrased it. My uncle was my best friend and my children's godfather, God bless his soul.

I wanted to be able to hold down one job that would support my children instead of having to contend with three different ones. I went from union bar to union bar with a steno pad – I had no resumés with me – and I wrote down what I thought that they might be looking for in an employee. In the end, I landed a job in a union bar that supported my family.

On the first night, the manager gave me the lowdown on the bar and what I was going to be doing. He told me that, at the end of each shift, we could have a free drink. I told him that I didn't drink; he said, "oh my, we've hired a failure". I didn't realize that you "had" to drink to work in a bar! How would I know? I'd lied to get the job… I told them what they wanted to hear. As it was union and I was on call, I sat by the phone every day, waiting for a call. It didn't take long. Many of the staff would get drunk and stoned, and so weren't able to come in. Before long, I was working 5 days a week – and they were upset that I wasn't sitting by the phone for days 6 and 7.

I was there for 5 years – until the owner assaulted me one night after the bar had closed. I called the bar manager but, somehow, he just didn't seem to get what I was saying. He may have been sleeping and I'd woken him with my call, I guess. The next day, he called me into his office; I explained everything that had happened and I quit on the spot. "Now what?", I thought to myself.

Well, nothing holds me back. I applied to go to college to take an accounting course. I was put on a waiting list to get in. A year later, my name came up on the waiting list; they called – and told me that they were no longer offering the course for which I had applied.

They did, however, offer me a place on an Insurance Fundamentals course; in completing the course, you receive a license to sell insurance. I was told that, if I wanted to come in and sit through the information session, I could. So, I went and listened – I even took an aptitude test. I had already taken an aptitude test at another college the week before and had passed with flying colors.

For the first test, I had been in a room by myself with large windows and plenty of room; for this one, though, I was in a room with 15 women, no windows, and the door closed. After I finished the aptitude test, the owner of the college called me into her office to tell me that I had passed – but barely. I could take the course but would have to study 5 times harder than anyone else in order to pass.

"Don't let a test define you."

My cousin had worked in insurance for a long time – since long before professionals were required to be licensed. I called to ask for her advice; my aunt answered the phone. She asked why I wanted to talk to my cousin, and I explained the scenario. In response, her exact words were: "If your cousin couldn't pass the insurance license exam, what makes you think you can?"

Are you kidding me? Not one but *two* people – in the space of a single afternoon – had told me that I couldn't do something. "No one tells me that I can't do something", I thought.

Fast forward 18 months: I'd not only taken the "Fundamentals of Insurance" exam but I'd passed – at the top of the class – without having to study anywhere near as much as the rest of my peers.

"Don't let someone's opinion of you to be your own."
"Believe that you are smart enough."

25 years into what is now a 36-year career in the insurance industry, I was talking to a customer, building a rapport with him. I asked him what he did for a living; he said that he worked in palliative care. I told him that I had always wanted to work in palliative care and that the reason that I was doing what I was currently doing is that several people had told me that I "couldn't". He laughed and said to me, "Don't you think that you've proven your point and that it's time to move on?". Now there's food for thought...

"Remember that jobs don't come looking for you."

I wasn't looking for a job – I already had one – when a new opportunity came looking for me. "Should I go to the interview?", I asked myself. I thought, "if I don't go, I will never know". That was 12 years ago, now, and was the best decision that I could have made; I love my job and career. I have the best staff and the most amazing customers.

You want to know what drove me? It was someone telling me that I wasn't good enough. There is something about someone telling you that you "can't" do something that gets those competitive juices flowing. In turn, that opens you up to new and exciting opportunities.

Everything that I did was to prove the naysayers wrong. My entire life, I have pushed myself to succeed to be the best version of myself – to excel at whatever I put my mind to.

"To my naysayers, I say, 'how do you like me now?!'"

I am here to tell you that you can take the negative seeds that people plant in your mind and decide what to do with them. It's your choice if you feed and nourish the seed and harvest the best life possible for yourself – or, if you're consumed by negativity, allow yourself to be overcome by your low self-esteem. Push that seed through all the manure – the negativity – and *flourish.*

Heather Scott

"We are women.
And women are warriors,
after all."

- Louise O'Neill -

5

MIXED BLESSINGS

TRUE CANADIANS

I was born in 1960, on the first day of Fall (the 21st of September). I was the second-born daughter to my father (a semi-professional basketball player and the youngest son in an Irish/Scottish family) and my mother (the eldest daughter in an English/Scottish family).

By the time that I was just 5 years old, they had separated. My mother, sister, and I relocated into an apartment, my mother made a living as a secretary. Soon afterwards, she met and married my step-father, adding him and his own three children to our family. My stepfather raised me and my sister as if we were his own. I quickly grew to think of him as my "true" father.

We lived in rural Surrey; it was quite different then from the city it is becoming today. At the time, it was comprised of people who came from predominately Caucasian/European backgrounds and cultures. There was a severe lack of students of color at my high school as well, perhaps just a handful, at most.

Growing up in the 1960's and 1970's meant that I lived at a time when almost everything seemed to be black and white, not just the televisions. JFK's rise to power, and assassination, together with the

MLK movement and accompanying upheaval, and most notably the Watts Rebellion and riots all had a massive impact on me as a young girl. The violence was both unbearable and unforgettable. At the time, I was not able to grasp the severity and the magnitude of the events that were unfolding before my very eyes. It was not until later in my life, upon reflection, that I was able to comprehend the influence that it had all had on me.

One of the first life-altering decisions that I had to make was shortly after I'd graduated from high school. I graduated as an honour student, despite having partied hard from a young age, went on to college to train to become a dental assistant. I was achieving straight A grades at college, when I was suddenly kicked out of my parent's house at the ripe old age of 18.

It seemed that my mother didn't like the fact that I could go out with my friends until the wee morning hours and, yet still maintain my straight A's at school. Since she was paying for it all, she decided that she had the right to control my life. I was subsequently forced to drop out of school and to get a job in order to support myself. I ended up securing a job in downtown Vancouver, and an apartment in Surrey on my own. By the time that I was 21, I was working as a bank teller, had made some friends for life, and was dating musicians, athletes, sailors... in short, I was "living my best life". I had no interest in having children or settling down. I just thought to myself, "these must be the good times that everyone sings about, why not just let them roll?"

Then at the age of 28, my life took another huge turn. I was playing softball at a tournament out of town when I met some guy from Coquitlam. He was the son of an African American basketball player from Louisiana, and a Chinese woman.

The next think you know, three months later, I'm pregnant with my first child. I didn't know this "boy" very well, so I gave him the option to either be a parent, actively involved in the child's life, or to simply walk away without having to accept any obligation or responsibility.

At the time, I was a credit reporter in Vancouver, and was, consequently, fully able to support myself and a child. Although the pregnancy had come as a surprise to me, I was excited and very willing to become a mother. My guy from Coquitlam decided to move in with me and to become a father.

Courtenay was born on August 11, 1989, at the Surrey Memorial Hospital. By this time, Surrey had become very culturally diverse. I recall the other women in the maternity ward asking me if Courtenay's father was East Indian, as she was definitely of mixed heritage, since we were in Surrey, they just assumed her father was East Indian.

I also recall a nurse telling me that she probably couldn't be discharged, as she looked jaundiced. I shot back at her that my daughter was "mixed" with Chinese.

Courtenay was a beautiful child. She slept through the night by the time she was 3 days old, and she thrived. She was very smart and reached all of her milestones early. When she was just 3 or 4 years old, I was contacted by a talent agent who worked in the Vancouver film industry and wanted to represent her professionally. She ended up starring in many commercials, having a few jobs on TB series, and during grade one she did Showboat at the Ford Centre for almost a year.

Several of the commercials that she worked on were for Fisher-Price, who hire children of a wide range of ethnicities in order to promote cultural diversity. Anyways, she was very popular in the industry as she had beautiful caramel-colored skin, and all at once represented black and white and Chinese cultures.

When Courtenay was about 9 months old, her father and I decided to get married. We moved to Maple Ridge, a small town on the outskirts of the Greater Vancouver area of British Columbia, and we bought a townhouse.

My second daughter, Sydney, was born on July 23, 1992, at the Surrey Memorial Hospital. She was not nearly as dark as her sister or my husband in terms of coloring. My husband looked at Sydney as if she were not his daughter because of how much lighter she was than him in skin tone.

However, there was absolutely no disputing her parentage, she looked identical to how he'd looked in his baby photos (just lighter) and I was no cheater. Sydney was a "mama's girl" from the start. She was quite different from her sister in every possible way. Courtenay was very much an extrovert, while Sydney, on the other hand, was much more introverted.

We sold the townhouse when Sydney was born and purchased a family house instead. Maple Ridge, at the time, was quite "small townish". We were probably the only mixed-raced family that lived there – something that I didn't even realize at the time.

I just remember people looking at me oddly, and strangers asking me whether the girls were actually my daughters. It upset me a lot, if you were to see my daughters, you'd know that they share many of my features. A lot of people who know us, say that they look a lot like me, only with a little more melanin.

The girls had very big, curly hair. This along with their caramel colored skin made them stand out. They were very smart, and well read but, I also believe that they felt that they had to be in order not to feel inferior to their peers at elementary school. Looking back, I feel that we were singled out in the community, there were no other families like ours in Maple Ridge at the time. We went through the "lice years" which, of course, were a complete and total nightmare for us due to the sheer amount of hair that both girls had.

As a result, braids became the norm for us, but that didn't stop the authorities at the school from picking on the girls for their hair. I had many altercations with the principal and often kept them home during lice breakouts, their hair could sometimes take up to 6 hours to check.

By 1998, my marriage was over. To put it simply, he was not the man I'd thought he was when I married him. I did not want my girls to think that it was acceptable to be with a man who didn't respect his wife or the mother of his children.

The relationship had become too much to bear any longer. I was the product of divorce, and I didn't want the girls to go through what I'd been through. I also realized that I wanted to get married in order to change my surname, so that it was the same as my children's. I had no real connection to my maiden name as it was my biological father's, it hadn't belonged to the man who I considered to be my real father.

One Saturday, when their father was at work, the girls and I secretly moved out to an apartment in the city. I'd had many discussions with him that had become violent on his part, I'd kicked him out of our home twice before due to anger issues. He would not leave permanently – so I did.

I left the house that I owned with only a few possessions just to get away. I quit my job and received a grant to return to the school from which I obtained my programming and web design degree. We struggled financially for years as I was not in receipt of any child support and could only work limited hours due to school. We struggled, but we made it.

I knew that people looked at us differently, as a family. Until recently – thanks to the "Black Lives Matter" movement, I was unaware of the internal struggles that my children must have faced during their adolescence. It is interesting that they identify most strongly with being black, when they're also of mixed Irish, Scottish, English, Métis, and Chinese heritage as well.

I am starting to gain a better understanding as to why though. For my girls, growing up in a very white suburban neighborhood, they were viewed as being black, and were treated as such. Had we relocated to a predominantly black or more ethnically diverse neighborhood, it might have been different (as a side note though, it's worth noting that there aren't really any predominately black neighborhoods in our area like those you'd find in the USA).

Sydney has become highly active in the Black Lives Matter movement, and I admire that. She's even made a point of sharing uncomfortable and obviously hurtful stories from her youth. One in particular was striking. She explained that the reason she'd worn braids in her hair for 4 years was that she'd wanted to hide her big, curly hair. At the time, I'd just believed that she was going through a "tomboy stage" and had thought nothing of it.

Reflecting on and being aware of what is currently happening around the world makes you realize that you just can't just put yourself in someone else's shoes, you can't possibly understand what it feels like to be a different color from your own. I don't feel like I grew up in a context of white privilege as I came from a "blue collar" working class, blended family and we had our own share of struggles. I remember when my mom remarried and my sister and I had to grow up with different surnames than our parents, brothers, sisters and that in itself is a weird situation to have to deal with as a young child.

We all have fears and challenges that we must face in life, some big, some small. Today, we have the 2020 pandemic, the highest rates of overdose deaths among the homeless, teen suicide appears to be more of a problem than ever, but the Blacks Lives Matter movement is, in my opinion, the most crucial issue at this time. It's a movement that's been ongoing for my whole life and I just turned 60!

In or around 2010, my eldest daughter, Courtenay, briefly worked as a receptionist at my place of employment. One day, a young

Caucasian man decided to direct some unkind racist words at my daughter (for which he was promptly fired). The episode was extremely uncomfortable for everyone but especially for my daughter.

My children have always been praised for their beauty - both (inside and out). I'm sure that it was very off putting for them to hear derogatory remarks about themselves, it would be for anyone).

I remember one incident when I was just 6 or 7 years old, I had a black baby doll named Mandy of all things. Having placed Mandy in the basket of my shiny, red bicycle as I rode it to school, I was excited to show her off for "show and tell". I remember telling my mother that, when I grew up, I was going to have "chocolate milk" babies. Maybe this was me driving my own destiny because I was right.

Approximately 6 years ago, my aunt and her partner researched our family history and learned that 5 generations back, one of the Scottish ancestors (my 5th great-grandfather) married a Métis woman from Manitoba. That revelation was yet another sign of our diverse family heritage.

I have always said when I was asked "what are your kids?" that they're true Canadians (Scottish, Irish, English, Black American, Chinese and Metis). Canada comprises all cultures, we all came from somewhere else and we are a truly diverse country.

My daughters are both grown women now. Courtenay is married to a wonderful man whose parents are Italian and Irish ancestry, we're looking forward to adding another culture to our family tree. Courtenay and her spouse have several businesses and are up in Northern British Columbia at this time.

Sydney is also with a wonderful man, they are just finding their path. Sydney also works on a podcast and has plans to return to school in the veterinary tech field.

In all, I have 2 very well-adjusted, incredibly unique daughters. I've been remarried to a great guy for 15 years and we now live on Vancouver Island, a beautiful place to retire, which I hope to do in the next 5 years. We have 2 black and white "tuxedo" cats, Marley and Sophie, and they're loving the big property.

Sharon Jones

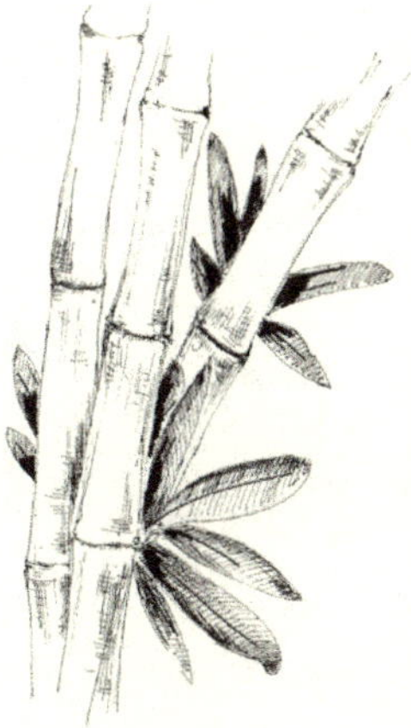

Plink
Plink
Plink
Plink
Plink
Green then
Yellow look skyward
Evocative query.

-Susan Harrison

6

PERCEPTION IS NOT ALWAYS REALITY

NOT RECOGNIZING THE BEAUTY INSIDE MYSELF

As I sit here and start to type out my "ugly" story, I'm reflecting on the fact that it's something that I've always felt. I've even looked up the meaning – of always feeling ugly. Of not measuring up to what other people think or expect of you. Of not seeing any beauty in myself.

This isn't a story in which the fairies come and – magically, overnight – a swan appears. This is a story about how I dealt with it – and still deal with it, every day of my life. My hope is that, in sharing my story, someone will see how silly I've been and, as a result, will be able to grow into and embrace the beautiful swan that lies within themselves.

Please note that, when I refer to feeling "ugly", I mean ugly in the most all-consuming sense of the term. Other than describing repulsive physical attributes, I also use the term to denote feelings of being stupid, uneducated, in the way, and unable to please.

It all started at home. I don't really know why. Looking back at my baby photos, I think that I was kind of cute looking. Although I've come a long way on my journey, it still turns my stomach to write that.

I was frequently compared with others. "Why aren't you pretty like so and so?". "Why aren't you smart like so and so?". I was told that I was just like my father – and would then be reminded of just how "bad" my father was. I didn't really know my father, at the time, I only knew that he was big and loud – and that he was someone who my grandmother didn't like.

At a young age, my mother had been tragically killed in a car accident. My father was unable to care for his six young girls on his own. So, my eldest three sisters stayed with my father – and I, together with my two younger sisters, was sent to live with other relatives. I grew up with my grandmother: my mother's mother.

Even before I'd started going to school, I was part of an exceptionally large yet close family. There were always cousins, aunts, uncles, and siblings around. It felt natural to have others around; I enjoyed my family. Many people from out of town would stop by as they were passing through. Grandma seemed to have the most sociable house of all; everyone liked to gather there.

However, as much as I loved my family – and perhaps because there were always so many kids around – for some reason, I was always the one who was teased and bullied. Maybe it's because I was ugly. I still couldn't tell you what made those kids want to hurt me so badly inside. To this day, I can hear them whispering "Yours Truly!": a silly name that they'd assigned me. Whenever I was around, they'd whisper and laugh. I craved their love and acceptance as a young child – but it just never happened. I was the outsider of the family who was habitually picked on by others.

I knew that my face was different. I had a full-face beard and moustache before the boys in my class had them. I was larger than everyone, taller by a foot. My breasts developed way before everyone else's. I was not encouraged to seek any help for this obvious "hormone issue". Nor did anyone talk to me or ask me anything about how overdeveloped I was at such a young age – not my grandmother, my teachers, my school counsellors, or other family members. I remember feeling lost, not knowing what to do. It was so confusing for me; I didn't understand why I was so different from the other kids.

When I was growing up, I had many adults in my life. They were all loving and caring but – for some reason – no one ever talked about my hormonal and physical problems. "Why?", I always wondered. "Why does no one seem to care?". I decided that it must be because I was ugly.

The teasing and bullying continued from my home life as I entered into my more advanced school years. Many of the children who I'd grown up with went to the same school as me. It didn't take long for the other children to catch on – to realize that it was okay to tease and bully me. Maybe it was because I was so ugly.

I did have one wonderful, supportive friend in school. Her name was Karen and, to this day, I still thank God for her. We became instant friends – and we still are. Even though I only had one friend in school, Karen was a lifesaver for me. She helped me to survive my school years.

When I left school, I was left with such an overwhelming sense of ugliness about myself that it has stayed with me ever since. I felt it so deeply that I could not shake it off. When you are teased and bullied for years as a child and as an adolescent, it kills something inside of you.

Relationships were pretty much non-existent for me as I went through my young adult life. I think I understand why; maybe it's because I was too ugly. I have a few stories that I could share – but they're still too hurtful to open up about. I couldn't entertain the idea that people would be interested in me. Even when anyone was genuinely interested in me, I pushed them away because I thought I was too embarrassing to be with. This has always been the way I've felt. I never felt that I was deserving of a relationship. I knew, deep down, that – if I were in a relationship – I would end up being hurt. And so, I avoided them.

As I've grown older, I've come to terms with who I am and who I've become. What do I do about my thoughts and feelings of ugliness? Every day, I tell myself that maybe I'm not ugly. Not as direct a manner as that – but in the context of the little things that I have happening in my life. I try to walk with my eyes up instead of fixed on the ground. This has been a challenge for a long time for me; I tend to look down when I approach people so that I can't see the looks of disgust on their faces. I hardly ever wear make-up or bother to do my hair. When people look at me, I don't want them to think that I'm trying to be something that I'm not. When I dress up, I feel like a fraud – like a freak.

When I hit the age of 40, things started to change for me – for the better. Finally, I felt brave enough to go and see a doctor. I needed to find out what had been happening to me all this time.

Finally, I discovered that I have a few medical conditions – ones that affect me emotionally as well as physically. I don't blame anyone for how I feel. However, had I known about these issues much earlier on, I think that I would have had the answers for myself and would have been better able to understand why I'm so different. With understanding and acceptance comes healing. I feel that my "healing" process could have started a lot sooner. But I'm so thankful that, even though it took until I turned 40 years of age, I've been able to discover what has plagued me throughout my entire life.

I think that the saying goes "if I had known then what I know now…"? Finding out that I have polycystic ovaries has brought such amazing relief to me. Some of the main symptoms of polycystic ovary syndrome (PCOS) are an inability to have children, an excess of male hormones, and obesity. That's me!

Knowing all of this hasn't, I should add, made it easier on me in terms of how I feel about myself. It has given me some relief, though: a reason as to why I was the way I was. I've found some relief in the knowledge that I no longer have to blame myself for all of my "ugliness". I understand, now, that I'm not some sort of freak.

There was a reason as to why I could never get pregnant – why I looked the way that I looked. Why it was so hard to lose weight. No matter how hard I tried, I couldn't lose weight. One year, I even went to the extreme of putting my fingers down my throat after eating. I'd tried many diets and other extreme methods of weight loss – but with no success. I'm still unable to lose more than a few pounds. I take medication that helps me with some of my problems – and I feel better because I have found acceptance. Because I know that there is a reason.

Overcoming negative feelings about myself by means of acceptance has been an instrumental factor; I have been hard on myself all these years. Because of the way I've treated myself, being so hard on myself, the process of trying to make simple changes is hard. Making changes in relation to how you feel about yourself is harder. Do feelings of ugliness go away? I don't think that they'll ever be completely gone. I can tell you that today, though, I'm doing so much better than I was before.

There are triggers – and there may always be triggers for me. When I think about something in a certain way or react in a certain way, I have to really talk to myself to avoid falling into feelings of despair. When I do that, I feel better about most of the things in my life – including myself.

I remember how, just recently, I was walking along and happened to pass two police cars. The officers were sitting in their respective cars, talking to each other through the car windows. One of them made a weird noise and they both started to laugh, immediately. I felt that they were laughing at me. My initial reaction was to feel bad about myself. All of the negative emotions from my past – of teasing and bullying – came flooding back, hard and fast. It took some serious talking to myself to convince myself that they were probably not talking about me or laughing at me. The positive thing is I did it. I gave myself a talking to and felt so much better for it. I told myself: "your perception is not necessarily reality".

I eventually met Ron: the love of my life; my husband. He lived right next door – who knew? I'd never pictured myself ever getting married – let alone standing in front of friends and family in a beautiful church, wearing an elegant, gorgeous dress. But there I was as a beautiful bride.

Smiling, hair done, beautiful dress (with a train). So far, that has been the best day of my life. My wedding is still being talked about as one of our family's favourite weddings. Everyone had so much fun – and they all told me just how beautiful Ron and I were that day.

My husband has a few medical concerns of his own. He has Marfan Syndrome. One of the characteristics of those who have the condition is long limbs. We joke that he was made for me; his long arms wrap around me for hugs. We love each other – with all of our flaws. Just like other couples. We all have flaws.

Ron calls me a "swan" – and I love that about him. He tells me that he loves me every day – and I also love that about him. I am blessed with two adult children and two wonderful granddaughters. Ron's family has accepted me; I'm treated as a beloved member of their family. Never – in my wildest dreams – did I think that I would become a grandmother! It is an immense pleasure in my life.

I have a job that I love and there is no teasing – or bullying – there. I wear dresses and feel good about myself. Still no make-up – though maybe one day? Or maybe not; it's not a concern for me. I'm okay with the way that I am.

Ron used to ask me, when we were first together, "why do you always say that you're ugly?". I'd always answer "because I am". Ron doesn't ask me that question very much anymore – because I'm now much kinder to myself and don't put myself down like I used to do.

If you're feeling the way that I always used to feel, please get some help. If you're older: so what? You still have many years left in your life; don't let the years go by feeling unhappy. There may be help out there for you as well. You'll never know until you reach out and investigate it for yourself. Don't be afraid; there's a certain peace that comes with knowing.

If there's anything in particular that I would want someone to take away from my story, it's this: we all have a hill to climb. The hill may always be steep – but it's still yours to climb and there's an amazing life to be found along the way.

Shelley Hatt

"My best
successes come
on the heels
of failure."

- Barbara Corcoran -

7

REINVENTING ME

LIVING WITH DEPRESSION AND CHRONIC PAIN – MY WAY

This is my story: my journey from being on top of the world to finding myself in a place of complete darkness and hopelessness – before finding my way back again.

I had moved from Nova Scotia to British Columbia with my daughter in 2002 in order for us to be able to start a new life together. It wasn't all roses – but I was determined to make the best life for us both. I wanted my daughter to have access to every possible opportunity in her future.

I didn't give up – no matter how difficult it was at times. I wanted to forge a successful career for myself to prove to myself – and to everyone else – that I could do it if I worked hard. And that's exactly what I did. I started off in a part-time job, working in a little tearoom. Then, a friend suggested that I look into working in real estate, saying that I'd be great at it. It turned out that I *was* great at it – until I wasn't.

September 26, 2011: the day that changed everything. "From this day forward, nothing will ever be the same": the words that resounded in my head clearly as I stared at the side of a semi-trailer.

Never did I think that those words would ever come to have such significance or in such a way.

Sitting in my car, I was in shock – wondering what had happened. What had I done? I prayed that the semi at which I was staring wouldn't move and drag me down the road. Still unsure as to what was going on, I turned around in my seat and saw that a car had smashed my back end. At that point, I realized that I had been in a car accident. All I could hear were the voices that were saying how hard I'd been hit – then sirens when the ambulance arrived, then those of the police.

The impact of the crash had been such that, when I'd snapped back into my seat – hitting my head with force on the headrest – I'd broken my seat. I'd come awfully close to going under the trailer of the semi. Luckily, though, my front end had hit its back tires, preventing me from doing so. I'd clearly had someone watching over me that day; it could have ended so much worse.

The ambulance attendants checked me out – but I refused to go to the hospital. Being a real estate agent, there was always work to be done; I was very dedicated to my job. I called my boss in hysterics and she arrived at the scene to collect me. She was quite surprised to find me in one piece, having seen the state of my car. Still in shock, all I could think of was the importance of finishing my work – the tasks that had been interrupted by the accident. I had two housing offers to deal with, a showing and the need to sort out the pictures for a new listing. Once those things had been accomplished, I felt that I should maybe then visit the hospital.

At the hospital, I was told that I had severe whiplash. I was advised to take two painkillers and to return to the hospital or to visit my doctor if my symptoms became worse. The next day, I decided to visit my doctor – who, immediately, signed me off work indefinitely. From there, a long process ensued.

Looking back, I really don't know how I did it. I was at the top of my real estate career; I was on fire and finally reaping the benefits of all my hard work. Nothing could stop me – or that's what I thought, at least.

The healing process felt like torture at times, trying to get my body back into shape. Everything from the top of my head to my lower back had been injured. My doctor started me off in physiotherapy right away. I had to have it a few times a week: stretching, pulling, exercising, acupuncture – you name it, they did it. My body felt like it had been ruined. I was plagued by headaches and nothing seemed to really help.

Just getting up every day was a challenge. Nothing was easy – and the prospect of driving had become something scary – but I knew that I had to make myself do it because my work required me to drive around all the time.

I found that I couldn't sleep; my mind just wouldn't shut down. All I could think of was the accident. I'd lie awake all night, watching TV, just hoping that I'd fall asleep.

The headaches were driving me crazy. One day, I started to hear a buzzing noise and thought that it must be coming from my neighbours. But no – it was in my head. Specifically, it was coming from my left ear. It'd come and go but then, at one point, it just stayed. At times, it was so loud that I couldn't make out any other sounds at all. It made me feel agitated. It was like having the ocean in my head 24/7 – except I wasn't on the beach, enjoying life. It turned out that I had developed tinnitus and some vertigo to go along with it.

I spent the next couple of months recovering. It was, though, just the beginning of an exceptionally long process: one which would end with a lot of self-medicating.

I spent my time doing everything that was suggested to me. As time went on, I started to notice – little by little – that things I'd always done were proving to be challenging. Something as simple as going for a walk, for instance; I could barely make it around the block. So, I started to do everything that was suggested to me for only a few minutes at a time. That way, I could work my way up to being able to manage these things for longer – when I did, though, I could still only manage for 20-30 minutes max. It was hard to believe that this was all I could manage without setting myself back for a couple of days. Walking up stairs, for example, was brutal. I felt like my legs were going to give up on me; once I'd finished climbing the stairs, I always had to sit down afterwards to take a break.

As each day passed with only minimal results, I was determined to have a breakthrough. Surely – if I kept doing whatever the doctor suggested – I'd start to feel better? Little did I know what kind of process it would all turn out to be. It was a long journey of having to try medication after medication to deal with the headaches, back and neck pain, nerve damage, and head injury. Pretty much everything from the top of my head to my lower back was affected.

Everything slowly started to go to shit – except that I didn't actually realize it. I kept thinking that I was going to have a full recovery, "time heals all", they say.

Finally, having been off work for a few months, my doctor gave me the all-clear to start back at work on a part-time basis. I was glad; now, I thought, I could get back into a routine and hopefully pick up where I'd left off. Or so I hoped, anyway.

The first day back seemed so strange – even foreign – to me. It felt really odd; I'd worked in real estate for a while. I was almost panic-stricken – but I convinced myself there was no problem. This, real estate, was what I did – what I do. I went along to my first appointment to show one of our listings. When I met with the other realtor and his client, the worst feeling came over me. It felt as though it was my first day in real estate; I felt dumbfounded and overwhelmed. I could hardly speak. Even though the other realtor was someone who I already knew, I suddenly became very self-conscious. Feeling worse by the second, I couldn't wait to get the hell out of there. I thought to myself, "geez, what's wrong with you? It's not like you – you've never done this before. No problem; it'll pass." But it didn't.

The road ahead was going to be difficult for me. As I continued to try to settle back into work, I found that I was still experiencing difficulties. I felt that I had to keep it all to myself, though; I didn't want my team to know that I was having problems. It would all eventually come to light, though, when I could no longer hide it.

I found myself struggling with all of my work. It was as though I were starting from the beginning; I couldn't remember how to complete my paperwork and I was forgetting things that I'd always remembered before. Even my thought process had changed to the extent that I had to double-check everything that I was doing. Little things irritated me no end. The noise in my ear started to really get to me. It never let up which did not help with my trouble focusing.

Driving to my appointments became a nightmare; I was terrified of having another accident. I would get so rattled in traffic that I started to suffer from anxiety and panic attacks – especially when I had to be close to transport trucks on the roads. A lot of the time, I had to make sure that I was driving with the windows right up; the sounds of the traffic all around me freaked me out. I was just a bag of nerves. It eventually reached the point where my daughter had to help me with my work by driving me to appointments. My daughter preferred to drive herself; it was too nerve wracking for her to travel in a car with me when I was behind the wheel. I took offence to that, asserting that I was a good driver; she quickly responded with "you used to be."

It didn't take long to figure out that driving or sitting for any length of time left me in a great deal of pain. It got to the point that I could hardly get out of the car because the pain was so bad. I also found standing very painful. As for climbing stairs – well, forget that. I had no option but to just suck it up, though, because my job involved those all the time. Painkillers and muscle relaxants became my best friends; I consumed them on a daily basis in order to simply get through the day.

As all of this continued, I realized that something just wasn't right. All the same, I carried on; I was sure that everything would sort itself out in time. It wasn't until I went to our company Christmas party that it all truly hit me. I found myself feeling completely overwhelmed and wanting to leave; I just couldn't handle having so many people around me – or the noise of it all. I just couldn't take all the chatter. I didn't want to have anything to do with these people – despite the fact that I knew all of them. I managed to stay just about long enough to have my meal. Then, I called my daughter – all freaked out – and asked her to come and get me straight away. At the time, I thought "okay, next time, it'll all be okay". But it didn't; it just got worse.

I didn't want to be around people – whether I knew them or not – which really was a problem in my line of work. By this point, I was seriously concerned, thinking "what the hell is wrong with me?". None of this was normal for me. I decided that I needed help as this was all getting to me and bringing me down.

I asked my doctor to refer me to a counsellor who I'd seen in the past when I'd been dealing with depression. The sad part, for me, was that I'd been in remission for 3 years: no drugs, nothing. Now, though, that process would begin all over again. Having to go back on medication and having to try to figure out what was going to work really sucked; anti-depressants take time to get into your system before kicking in. Having to go down this road again when everything had been going so well in my life – especially with my career – was a bitter pill to swallow.

All I could do was try to just keep doing what needed to be done to get everything back to normal as best as I could. "Normal" would never return, though. I just kept getting up every day and carrying on with my appointments: physiotherapy, counselling, massage, chiropractic treatments, and work.

Then, on top of everything else, I had to hire a lawyer. I knew that I wouldn't be able to handle the fight that lay ahead of me, because of the car accident, on my own. I needed someone to do that on my behalf so that I could focus solely on getting better. Honestly? I didn't have a lot of fight left in me. My time and energy had become consumed by endless medical appointments; I had about eight of them every month – sometimes more.

Hiring a lawyer, though, just led to more appointments. I had to meet with specialists in relation to my case. The insurance company, too, sent me to meet with their own specialists. This was all while I was having to prepare for my case. Travelling into Vancouver for legal appointments and meetings with specialists was a nightmare for me; I had to take transit service. They were long, painful trips for me. I couldn't drive myself – I was too terrified to do so.

Trying to work against the backdrop of all of this was a challenge. I was so dedicated to my work that I didn't want to let anyone down. Eventually, though, indulging that mentality would come at a cost. Every day just kept getting harder and harder, leading to minimal results despite my best efforts. I finally started to embrace the "fake it until you make it" theory. I couldn't really talk about it all to my co-workers as I didn't want them to know just how bad everything really was. I just did what I had to in order to manage my pain on a daily basis – whether that involved relying on medication or self-medicating to try to find any kind of relief.

Everything felt so overwhelming and so hopeless that talking about it didn't really help. No one could understand the pain that I was dealing with both physically and mentally. If you don't look broken, they don't get it. The frustrating part was trying to explain it all, only to find my words were falling on deaf ears. I honestly couldn't handle one more person saying "get over it", "move on", "you just have to be positive". If it were that easy, I would have been fixed a long time ago – tell me something I don't know.

I kept trying to "fight the good fight" but, over time, found that I was getting beaten down. I found myself starting to lose hope. I was getting tired of trying stuff: more medications, more rehab, more appointments. If felt never-ending. I tried to focus on my faith more by reading self-help books – anything that might help me in my efforts to try to stay positive.

I started to drink more to try to escape from the pain and suffering. I thought that it might help me to forget about everything that had happened – temporarily, at least – but that really didn't work other than leaving me hungover. I just couldn't stop the car accident from plaguing my thoughts. I slowly began to slip down a dark rabbit hole; I could no longer see the light at the end of the tunnel. I stopped caring about myself or my work – about anything, really – and it started to show.

I no longer cared about my appearance – something in which I'd always taken pride. Everything became hard work. On top of all of that, my health in general started to go downhill. I couldn't get my blood pressure under control, pain management became more challenging, and so on.

Work started to go downhill. I stopped caring about whether or not I was able to secure any business – and that eventually became quite clear to my team. The flame had finally gone out. That was the end of my career as I knew it. All of my hard work, the endless hours that I'd put in so as to make a good life for my daughter and I – gone. Now, I had no chance of ever winning a sales award – something that, before the accident, I'd been so close to achieving. Everything had just gone to shit. I was devastated yet, at the same time, relieved that I no longer had to "fake it until I make it".

That triggered a whole other phase of feelings that I had to work through. It was almost as though I were mourning a death. I felt like I was stuck in this whirlpool that was endlessly going around and around me, praying that I'd eventually be sucked into this hole, never to return. Amidst all of the turmoil, I hadn't yet processed the fact that my daughter had gone off to university. We'd been like two peas in a pod – and on our own, just the two of us – for so long. Going away was probably the best thing that she could have done – getting away from me before I destroyed our relationship. I was self-destructing.

I was completely alone – or, at least, that is what it felt like. I felt like I had the weight of the world on my shoulders, trying to deal with depression, chronic pain, PTSD, unemployment – oh, and diabetes had been added into the mix, too. I was having to try to deal with levels of stress that I had never encountered before. I was also having to try to deal with my lawsuit. Thank goodness, though, that I had a really good lawyer who could handle all the legal aspects. For everything else, I had my counsellor.

My counsellor was my angel – always there to talk me through things and to help me to pick up the pieces after my meltdown. Believe me: there were lots of those. Without work, everything really started to unravel. I didn't really care – but I knew that I had to try to find work of some sort in order to keep a roof over my head. I managed to secure a part-time job but, in the end, I just couldn't do it. It was physically too hard for me. I couldn't handle being on my feet all day; my back just wouldn't take it. By this time, slowly but surely, everything was grinding me down. Some days, I didn't even know what would set my back off.

The simplest things became challenges: cooking, cleaning, walking… my joy was slowly slipping away. I started to stay in my condo more and more. I felt that I was at least safe there, not having to worry about having another car accident. This accident had left me not wanting to drive and feeling paranoid. I didn't even want to socialize with friends. By avoiding them, I didn't have to explain anything. Being by myself prevented all of that – but it eventually led to my becoming a hermit. I spent a lot of time drinking; it was the best pain relief and my form of escape, together with watching TV and surfing the web.

I lost myself by watching TV. In doing so, I could transport myself to different worlds. I found myself crying all of the time, though, and prayed that God would just take me. I felt that I was past the point where things could get better. I just couldn't accept that this was what my life was going to be like from now on. I'd been told that, when the pain was under control, the depression would be better. That's the best advice that a shrink could offer me in a 15-minute session.

I tried so many different forms of medication to control the pain – even oxy. But, in the end, I thought "hell no"; I wasn't going to add "addict" to the mix. I was so sick and tired of being sick and tired; no wonder I'd been slipping down the rabbit hole. As if all of the rehabilitation, doctors' appointments and therapy weren't enough to deal with, I was facing the very real possibility of losing my home. I just didn't know how much more I could deal with. It was taking forever to settle my lawsuit, too.

No one will ever know the anguish that I was going through. It was so bad that I felt that I just wanted to die; I thought that it would be the only way in which I would find peace. I became numb to everything. "Do this", "try that", "let's whip her into shape"; that's all it seemed that anyone was interested in.

The faster they could fix me, the less money that the insurance company would have to fork out. They even went as far as retraining me to try to get me back into the workplace.

I decided to train for the position of Pharmacy Assistant, thinking that it would be a good choice; I'd worked in a drug store before, so I already had a lot of relevant experience. In the end, though, it would prove to be a big mistake. Off to college I went, though, which turned out to be the worst nine months ever. It was then that I began to realize that my brain just wasn't working quite right. I brushed it off, though, attributing those strange feelings to stress, age, etc. I don't even know how I made it through that course; the pain that I was experiencing every day was horrible.

I had to take transit service to get to school as I didn't want to drive. So, from start to finish, I was putting in an almost 12-hour day. I always studied in the morning before class as my brain and body were mush by the end of the day. Despite all the pain and tears, I managed to graduate. Now would be the real test as to whether or not I could find work. I hoped that I'd be able to remember what I'd learned.

I did find a job – one that was really close to home. It was perfectly situated; it meant that I didn't have to travel and, as a result, incurred fewer expenses. That was just as well; I didn't have two cents to rub together. It didn't take long for me to figure out just how bad everything was, though. Three to four hours into my 8-hour day, I found that I was in so much pain from standing that I became fearful that my legs were simply going to give way. I experienced difficulties with focusing, answering the phone, waiting on customers… I couldn't remember anything and my brain just couldn't process information in the way that it had done before.

I started to feel very discouraged. It was taking me so long to come to grips with things. Normally, I'd pick things up after just a couple of tries; now, it was taking me seven or eight attempts. I just didn't get it; I knew that I wouldn't make it past my probation period at my job. Ironically, the very day that I went for arbitration to settle my case – six years later – I was let go from the pharmacy. It was good timing.

After having spent the day in Vancouver with my lawyer, trying to hash out a deal with the insurance company, the matter was finally brought to a close. What a relief. I felt so relieved, knowing that I'd prevented my home from being foreclosed on. I'd be able to pay off my debts and move on. It was all so surreal. It was over. I was in a daze by the time that I got home – but it was nothing that a drink couldn't fix.

I decided that it was time for me to move back to Nova Scotia where I'd have more of a support system around me. I knew that I had to leave; there were just too many reminders of what I'd lost. Everything reminded me of the car accident. I knew that it would be hard to leave the dear friends that I'd made during the 15 years that I'd lived there.

I finally started to feel hopeful. The thought of being reunited with my old friends was an exciting one. I'd been given a second chance to start over. It didn't take me long to set things in motion, like booking a flight home and starting to house-hunt. I needed to buy a new place before putting my current home on the market as I knew that the latter wouldn't take long to sell. Indeed, within a week or so, I'd sold it. I packed everything up and headed back to Nova Scotia.

I was so excited about my new lease on life. Finally, I thought, everything would go back to normal. I expected a miracle – that I'd be healed, just like that. That's not, of course, what happened; I found myself in a downward spiral once again.

After all of the stress of everything that had come before had been released – and after all of my excitement of being home and in my new place had worn off – I felt all the energy leave my body. I just wanted to hide away. I knew that I needed to get my support system in place – I needed to find a doctor and a chiropractor, for instance. I hoped that my former doctor, from when I'd previously lived here, would take me back as a patient – and, fortunately, she did. That was the first thing that I needed to do: see her and get my health back on track. I needed to bring her up to speed about everything that I'd been dealing with. Once again, we'd have to figure out which medication might work best. I was hopeful that she'd have some other, better ideas, too.

The one thing that did work for me was cannabis. That had been identified as a last resort by my previous doctor – but we'd run out of options. He'd been right in asserting that it would work – it did – I just had to get my current doctor to prescribe it for me. It wasn't as accessible here as it had been in British Columbia. I felt hopeful, in one sense, that I was getting things sorted – but I was still severely depressed and wondered how I was going to be able to function. I could no longer "fake it until I make it". I wondered why I was still like this. "I should be happy", I thought. "I should be out there enjoying life". Why hadn't I had my miracle?

I explained all of this to my doctor. I was at my wits end with it all. How would I ever be able to work – or do anything, for that matter? She said she knew of a psychiatrist who worked wonders with patients who were in the same place as me. She asserted that I needed to see him. The only catch was that I would have to wait about a year to see him as he was so busy. Well – that was the last thing I wanted to hear. I thought to myself, "I'll never make it that long in this state".

That was the longest year I've ever had to wait. Thank heavens that I still had my counsellor from British Columbia to talk to once a month.

I just tried to do my best each day, pushing myself to move forward. Some days, I didn't manage to do that quite so much. I still found it difficult to socialize and to be around people – even those I knew. I found socializing painful to the extent that being around groups of people – their chatter and their sounds – irritated me so much that I'd have to leave. I felt like a loose cannon, not knowing what would set me off. I often withdrew, wanting to be left alone. I found it hard to carry around all of these feelings and didn't want to be a "Debbie Downer" and burden my friends. After a while, you worry that you're just sounding like a broken record.

I'd lost all sense of joy about the stuff that I'd once loved to do and no longer did. No matter how hard I'd tried, nothing had changed since I'd moved home. Realizing that just pushed me a little further down the rabbit hole. Then, to add salt to my wounds, I ended up sustaining a second head injury when I fell and smashed my head on the pavement. No wonder I wanted to die.

Thoughts of suicide started to creep back into the corners of my mind. With each passing day, it all just got worse. I finally began to understand why people committed suicide. It all became very clear. If this was as good as it was going to get, it certainly wasn't how I was going to spend the rest of my life.

The bad days outweighed the good ones. I started to put a plan together for how I was going to leave this painful world in which I found myself. I started to find peace, knowing that death would grant me release – freedom. My plan was a simple one. I would write a letter to my daughter and my friend, explaining that I could no longer carry the burdens and pain that had worn me down. Then, I would take an enormous amount of pills – ones that I had been saving over time. The end.

The day finally came when I received the call to say that I could start sessions with my new psychiatrist. I felt hopeful and helpless at the same time; I couldn't imagine what he'd be able to do for me.

I hadn't reached this point overnight and nothing was about to change overnight, either. I'd have two sessions a month as I was in dire straits. The psychiatrist asked me to identify the first thing that I wanted to address in my sessions. It was, of course, the suicidal mode in which I'd found myself. He agreed that I needed to get off the suicide train and back onto the platform that I loved – that was the analogy that he used to describe it.

I wasn't convinced that anything was going to work as I felt that I'd already tried everything. He said that there's always something else to try. He said that, if he thought there weren't, he'd agree with me and say "yes, suicide is the only way out". He asked me to do this exercise where I had to count how many times a day I thought about suicide and then record that number every day for a month. I couldn't believe that I'd thought about it 158 times; I hadn't realized just how much it was consuming me.

The more I became aware of my thoughts, the more I realized just how much work I was creating and how much time I was wasting in my life. These thoughts were draining me of energy that I didn't have. After that, I started to feel more in control of my thoughts. I'd finally made it onto the platform and was watching the suicide train fly by – and I wasn't on it any longer. I finally started to believe that there just may be hope for me.

Breaking down all of the components that were destroying my life, piece by piece, made it easier to go forward. Working on my suicidal thoughts was just the tip of the iceberg in the context of my healing process – but it was the most important one. I considered it to be a huge accomplishment for me. It was hard going through this process in itself; I just wanted to be free and at peace – something that I hadn't experienced for a very long time. It was hard to accept the life that I had been dealt. I still believed that I would be able to do everything that I wanted to do.

I thought that I'd be able to undertake physical work, for example. Whenever I tried, though, I just ended up in pain – agony – for days. Being stubborn, though, I just kept trying. But I eventually reached a point where I didn't want to do anything. Simply getting up each day was hard enough. On top of it all, I still had to find work and learn to deal with being around people.

My psychiatrist gave me some really good suggestions in terms of strategies that I could use to try to overcome my issues. To get back into the habit of accomplishing small daily tasks, we used the 10-minute rule: I'd decide on work that needed to be done and would focus on doing it for 10 minutes. If I really couldn't complete the task, then that was okay; I could try again later on. Adopting this technique alleviated the pressure and guilt that I felt each day for doing nothing. I actually began to accomplish things. I managed to get work done each day by using this method. In doing so, I began to feel liberated from my feeling of guilt; I knew that it was okay if I didn't do anything.

Then, we started working on my people issues. I would force myself to visit places where I knew that there would be groups of people – like big events – and I'd stay for short periods of time until I felt comfortable being there. The more I practiced, the better it became; I always knew that I had the option of leaving it if all became too much for me. Even while doing this, I knew that I didn't want to deal with people 24/7. I also knew that I would no longer fit into the regular workplace. That realization left me feeling discouraged; I just didn't know what I was going to do – but what I did know was that I couldn't live off of my savings forever. I was still quite a few years away from being able to retire. I was actually starting to make progress with things that started to boost my confidence, making me want to keep trying. That desire to persevere was something that I hadn't felt in a while.

Thanks to my newfound confidence, I had the courage to reach out to my local employment center for help. I just knew that there had to be something out there that I could do without having to deal with people all of the time. I knew that most of the jobs that I could apply for would be in the retail sector – and that, as such, they wouldn't be suitable. I also wanted to work within my local community rather than having to travel; I didn't want to drive any distance. I also had to find something that wasn't going to involve my having to take a course – there was no way that I was going to put myself through that again. I didn't want to have to do anything that was going to require a lot of brainpower. So, in short, it was a tall order to fill.

Having brainstormed ideas with my caseworker at the employment center, we came up with the idea of self-employment. By starting my own project, I would have the ability to work on my own terms – and that would work well in the context of my current issues. I knew that I liked older people and got along well with them – so the idea of becoming a private caregiver seemed to be a good fit.

So, my new journey began. I was accepted into a self-employment program and started to put together a business plan. It was sure to be a challenge for me – but, with the support of friends and family, and with my counsellor and my psychiatrist in my corner, I stood a chance of making it all happen. As everything started to move forward with both my business and my health, which was improving, I came to learn that acceptance would prove to be the key. Once I'd accepted that I had limitations and that I was the best I was going to be – and that it was okay to not be okay – it was a bit easier for me. That mentality made all the difference.

I started to accept that it was okay to say no to things if I didn't want to do specific tasks or go to certain places. I also accepted the fact that it was okay if I was no longer interested in past hobbies or just couldn't do what I'd always been able to do before. I could find new things that would bring joy into my life – and that was all okay.

While trying to navigate all of this chaos in my life, I reinvented myself. I became the best possible version of myself. I finally felt like I had some normality in my life once more – and I had a career again.

Working with seniors would prove to be my calling – my purpose. I have the ability to be compassionate and caring, especially when it comes to working with individuals who are suffering from Alzheimer's. I, too, know what if feels like to be broken. When one has Alzheimer's, you basically feel as though your brain is broken and no longer works the same as it once did. That was how things had felt for me for some time. I never thought that I'd be able to make it to this point where I finally feel normal and work in a role that brings me so much joy and fulfillment.

What I've learned from this journey is that it is in your deepest darkest moments that you learn and grow the most. I've learned that it's okay to not be okay. I've learned that you can reinvent yourself – and that acceptance is the key. Once you've learned to accept the things that you cannot change, the healing begins. You don't have to "fake it until you make it" – and there is no shame in reaching out for help. Just remember that there's always something that hasn't been tried and that, no matter how hard it gets, there's always hope. Don't give up. I found my strength through my belief in God.

I'm not 100% well again, nor am I ever likely to be, but I'm at peace with where I am. I've come a long way – which is all you can hope for. I'm proud of myself and I treasure every good day I have. I can never know what each day will be like – but I try not to dwell on such thoughts. At the end of the day, I shut my mind down by telling myself that there's nothing that can be done at this moment in time and that tomorrow is another day.

My story gives you a glimpse of what it's like to suffer from depression and chronic pain. If what I've written here helps just one person, then this endeavour has been worth it. I'm proud of myself for being able to tell my story. It hasn't been easy, having to relive it all. Now, I want to try to put my story up on the shelf – and leave it there.

Susan Daborn

Aqua ambrosia
blue ripples composed, still, deep,
transport thee to me.

-Susan Harrison

8

LOVE AND FAMILY

NEVER STOP LEARNING

Growing up, I had everything I ever wanted or needed. I was raised by two loving parents, both of whom were teachers. My mom was a grade three teacher, and my father was the principal of an elementary school as well as being its music teacher.

I had two older sisters. Throughout our childhood, we would take vacations to the Shuswap Lake where we had a cabin; we spent our summers there. We would spend the days at the beach and made a lot of friends who we would catch up with every summer.

The very first house that I remember us living in was in Saanich, British Columbia. There were acres of forest in the backyard. To this day, I can still remember carving a heart into the beautiful arbutus tree in the yard. While its shell was a deep red, when carved, it revealed a cream color beneath. Our mother would pack our lunches for us in brown paper bags and we would venture out into the forest and onto our neighbors' farm, riding their cows and staying out until darkness fell and the streetlights came on.

As the years went by and my older sister reached the age of 14, she left home and never came back. I didn't know – I didn't understand

– why she had gone. I only knew that I missed her very much as we were the closest of the siblings; she would pick on the middle sister and protect me from her when we would fight.

We then moved to a house in Sydney where we were closer to my mother's elementary school. This house had a pool right in the middle of it. When my second sister turned 14, she also left home, never to be heard from again.

So, both of my siblings had now gone – and I wasn't sure why they had left me. I was 13 by this point and my parents kept me busy with lots of activities: swimming, track, field – and I was also a professional springboard diver. I even had the opportunity to compete in the Commonwealth Games for springboard diving, achieving 8th place.

At this time in my life, I was happy and thought that I "had it all". I had no worries, no struggles; I was just enjoying everything that I had around me. I was missing just one thing, though: my sisters. I didn't understand why they'd gone – and why they hadn't come back. My parents kept saying "you will leave us next". I didn't understand what they meant but just assured them "no, I promise I will never leave."

One day, when I was in school, I was called to the principal's office, having been informed that there was a phone call for me. As I picked up the phone, I heard my eldest sister on the other end of the line. She asked me "Do you want to live with me and meet your real mother?" I was at once both confused and happy – I was so happy just to hear her voice once more. She said that she was at the end of the street on which my school was situated and would take me with her.

Without even thinking, I left the school and met both my sister and her husband at the end of the street. She explained to me that the people who had raised us were not our real parents; we had been adopted. I was shocked and confused but, still, incredibly happy just to see my sister again. I left with her that day and never looked back – breaking the promise that I had made to my parents.

My eldest sister drove me to Saskatchewan to meet my birth mother. She also told me that my other sister was there as well, living with our biological mother. At that point, I understood why both of my siblings had left me; they had come to live with their birth mother. The car ride to Saskatchewan seemed to take forever. There was so much snow and ice that we even accidentally hit an elk with our car on the journey. I was very scared.

When we finally reached the city of Moose Jaw in Saskatchewan, we pulled up in front of a house. There, I saw my second sister – as well as the lady who turned out to be my birth mother. I didn't know what to think, or how to act, or what to feel. I called my adoptive parents and told them where I was – but I have never asked them why they had not told me the truth. I was, quite simply, just happy to be with my siblings once more.

I lived with my birth mother for a year. By the end of that single year, both of my sisters were married and had moved out of our birth mother's home. Although I was still attending a school, I was no longer participating in sports: no more swimming, no more diving. It was a very different way of life. My birth mother was poor and in receipt of forms of income assistance. She did not work. Things were so stretched that we had to ask before taking anything from the fridge. I wasn't at all used to this way of living.

One day, when I came home from school, my birth mother informed me that we were moving to Vancouver, British Columbia. She said that there was a job opportunity for her, there, and that she had family members there who were ill and needed help. She sold everything that we had in the house, packed all our clothing into the car, and set off in the car for Vancouver. On our arrival there, we moved into an apartment, and my sisters eventually moved there, too, with their husbands.

I was in high school when I met my first boyfriend. I ended up getting pregnant at 16. My relationship with my boyfriend did not last, though; he did not believe that he was the father of my child. So, I remained living with my birth mother and she helped me to raise my son. I dropped out of school once I'd reached grade 10.

After that, we moved from the apartment into a house; we needed more room. It was then that I met the most charming, sophisticated man imaginable. He worked at his uncle's gas station – which was close to my mom's house. I made sure that I went to the gas station every single day to buy some cigarettes and to fill up on gas. This man was very good-looking, well-dressed, and had an attractive accent. He knew exactly what to do and what to say to woo me; he charmed his way into my heart.

When he eventually asked me for coffee, I told him about my son. His reply was "that is fine, I just want your heart and your mind". He told me that he was from Palestine and that he had been forced to move to Lebanon at a young age in an effort to escape the war – even though there was, as it turned out, also war in Lebanon when he was growing up. I really felt for him when he told me about his past and what he had gone through.

At the time, I was young and foolish; I didn't understand what he meant when he said that he wanted my heart and mind. It was the first red flag that I ignored. Nonetheless, I told him that he could have my heart but not my mind.

I was 17, he was 23, and we were in love. We ended up getting married 3 months later and we moved into his house. My birth mother was happy that she didn't have to support me and my child any longer. My husband had another job, working at the Glazier Union, and he really took care of both me and my son. We were happy for a while and we even had three more children together. I was 23 years old with 4 small children and staying home while my husband worked.

Over the course of the next few years, he brought his mother and father from Lebanon – as well as his two brothers – to live with us. We bought a bigger house into which we all moved as an extended family. It was a nine-bedroom house, so everyone had a room; there was even a backyard that had a swing set for the kids. We bought our own gas station, and all of the family went on to work there, even my sisters and his brothers.

As the years went by, I began to feel overwhelmed by the pressure that was being placed on me and my children as a result of his demands and those of his family. I was working, too, at the gas station as well as cleaning the house, taking care of the children – and his parents – as well as being ordered around by his brothers. They would tell me what I was allowed to do and not allowed to do when my husband was out working three jobs in order to take care of everyone. I was losing my hair because of the stress; I had ulcers that were so painful that I knew that something needed to change. I was depressed and stayed in my room with the children; my mother-in-law would scream if the kids made what she considered to be too much noise.

So, I asked my husband if we could have our own house – a place for just me, him, and the children – but he refused, saying "we all live together, we are all one, this is the way we do things". He became abusive toward me. The last straw was when there was a particular incident when we were having an argument. I'd shut the bedroom door – but he kicked the bedroom door down and came running into the bedroom, slapping me, open-handed, and repeatedly. His mother came in and lay on top of me in an effort to prevent him from hitting me – but this did not stop him. I was scared for myself and the children, and so I called 911. My husband was arrested and taken away from the house. I packed a few bags and left with my children; we went to my sister's house.

My sister took me to the hospital where I was told that I had a concussion in addition to having multiple bruises. I lived in poverty for two years with my four children. Financially, I was living off income assistance and child tax payments. The courts ordered him to pay me child support and alimony – but I didn't get one penny from him. I didn't want my children to suffer the way that I had suffered while living with my birth mother in a low-income house, barely able to eat and survive, and so I decided to let him have the children if he remarried. So it was that the children moved back in with him – and his new wife, and his mom, and his dad, and his brothers. They all lived together. I, meanwhile, would see my children every second weekend; the rest of the time, they were with their father.

At this point, I decided to go back to school to study cosmetology; I have always had a passion for hair and for helping people. I also wanted to educate myself as I had not graduated from high school. I went to hairdressing school and received my certificate within a year. Having spent years working in salons and watching the children grow, it was incredibly satisfying to finally be able to financially support myself and to accomplish this goal.

My ex-husband had three more children with his new wife over the next few years. I treated them as though they were my own when I visited. Then, there came a point at which my ex-husband decided to move to London Ontario with all of his family. Almost a year after they'd been there, though, I received a phone call; my ex-husband's new wife had left him, taking their three children to Lebanon with her.

On one occasion, my ex-husband became upset and struck my eldest daughter. She told the school. He had to leave the house and asked me to come and pick up my three children. I flew there, retrieved my children, and returned to Vancouver.

My ex-husband flew to Lebanon. Because of the cultural norms there, he had more power against his wife; he took their three children from her and flew to Dubai. He then called me, crying, saying that he was going to kill himself and that he didn't know what to do.

He wailed that he had three small children with him and that he didn't want to live as he was. I told him to come back to Vancouver and said, "move in with me, I will help you and we will raise all of the children together".

So, we got a small rancher. With all seven children, we were together once again. He was not working at this time; I was working as an administrator at an electrical company as well as styling people's hair either from home or by providing a mobile service.

One day, after I had been out to help a friend move from Edmonton to Vancouver, I had returned home to find that he was gone – and so were the children. He told me over the phone that he couldn't stay living with me while receiving no affection from me. I explained that I was simply exhausted from working, cleaning, and cooking – I was so tired by the end of the day – but he didn't understand. He took the children back to our old house and stayed there for a while before eventually bringing his second wife back from Lebanon.

I wasn't aware that he had been talking with her – and I was done fighting with him. I also refused to be his second choice. I was very surprised that they were back together, but I was also happy for their children that they would have their mother back in their lives. He supported her financially through nursing school and they moved into a co-op; she had made it clear that she did not want to live with his mother, father, and brothers again.

They lived there for 3 years until, one day, she left again, leaving their children hurting. I knew that I could not get back together with him – but I did take responsibility for all of their children as none of it was their fault and I loved them all. Over the years, I couldn't bear to miss out on anything including all of the hospital visits, the broken bones, the surgeries, the volleyball games, the soccer games, the basketball games, the music concerts, choir…

I attended all of these activities for the children's sake – that's what kept me going. I was being needed and wanted by all of the children. I was still working as a hairdresser but, over the years, it had taken a toll on my body. I had developed back pain and golfer's elbow / tennis elbow and could no longer do the job that I loved. I decided to research what else I could do.

My children were growing up and they didn't need me as much as they once did. So, I decided to go back to school. I remember my instructor from hair school fondly and decided to talk to her about how she started to be an instructor. It was the absolute best meeting that I could have hoped for – and it opened my eyes to a wonderful career. I took the Provincial Instructor Diploma Program (PIDP) at Vancouver Career College (VCC) so that I could remain in the same industry but teach the skills instead of using them in practice.

It was a 6-month course – and I gave up a few times along the way – but my children encouraged me and kept me going. They proof-read my essays and helped me to find the right words when I couldn't find the words to put on paper. They were, and are, my backbone. They are the ones who saved me mentally and physically. I am truly blessed. They also have taught me to put myself first – because, if I don't take care of me, I can't help anyone else. I have learned to say "no" to certain things – and, crucially, that it's okay to say "no".

I've learned that it's important not to overload myself and to take the quiet time for myself that I need in order to recharge. Most of all, I have learned the value of setting boundaries with people and limiting the access that they have to you. Be kind, be honest, and be self-loving. One Love.

Theresa Waugh

"Life is not measured by the number of breaths we take, but by the moments that take our breath away"

- Maya Angelou -

9

JAIMIE REBECCA

MEMOIRS OF A PREEMIE

I was 20 years old in the summer of 1990 and living a party life with my two sisters as roommates and I had a new boyfriend I loved. I was going along having a grand old time. Then, however, I was hit by some shocking news: I was pregnant. I had been dating my boyfriend for only a few months at that time and was certainly not prepared for what was to come.

I was young and scared but also strong and independent, so I knew that I could do this, with or without my boyfriend's support as I wasn't sure how he would react to the news. There was never a thought of not having her or giving her up for adoption. What I was not prepared for, and no one could be, was going into labor just 24 weeks into my pregnancy.

With my boyfriend by my side I went to the emergency room at Burnaby General Hospital and the staff went to work immediately. I remember so clearly one labor and delivery nurse telling us, "your baby is going to be a peanut.". She was going to be born no matter what they did, so I was transferred to Grace Hospital in Vancouver, which is attached to Children's Hospital so that the baby would receive immediate attention when she was born.

I was transferred by ambulance with my doctor riding in the back with me the whole way. She was young, and this was her first premature delivery. It was pretty amazing how she supported us through the labor. I was admitted and given drugs to stop the labor. They did what they could to stop the labor but, like I said she was coming, so in the end I delivered a 24-week-old peanut.

I wrote her story in the following journal in real time, every day of her life. One note, the pronoun "they" refers to the members of the hospital staff, the doctors, nurses, therapists, and so on.

Tuesday, November 20, 1991

I was born at Grace Hospital in Vancouver, BC, at 11:29 p.m. Tuesday, November 20. Mom and dad sure weren't expecting me so soon. I was very tiny, just one pound and ten ounces. The doctor who delivered me was Dr. Jackson and the people from Children's Hospital were there to take care of me. Daddy saw me when I was born, but mom missed it. I can't open my eyes and it's hard to breathe but I'm here. I cried when I was born and moved around a bit.

Day 1 - Wednesday, November 21

I'm in an incubator, and everyone is very worried, but I had a good day. Mom and dad both came to visit, and I held onto mom's hand. After mom and dad left in the evening, I started to have problems with my lungs, though, and they had to put tubes in my right one. I think that they must be giving me drugs because I feel very relaxed. The doctors and nurses seem to think I might not make it through the night tonight. My blood sugar is high, and my temp is low.

Day 2 - Thursday, November 22

Well I made it! My vitals are all back up, but I'm still drugged. They warmed me up a lot and I feel better. Mom came in the morning, but I could not touch her too much. I'm too relaxed to move. They say I'm having a bit of a problem with my heart; a blood vessel didn't close when it should have so they are giving me more drugs to fix it.

Mom and dad came back tonight, and I was very happy to see them. I love them both very much. Mom said she was leaving the hospital today and going home with daddy. I wonder where home is?

Day 3 - Friday, November 23

I'm still here and doing great! They fixed my little heart problem and probably will take the tubes out of my lung tomorrow. I had an ultrasound on my brain to see if I'm bleeding and that turned out fine. My nurse Liz says that she knows I'll be okay. I know it too.

Mommy came to visit, and I held her hand. They decreased my morphine level so I'm more active. They have a blue light on me, it keeps me warm and stops jaundice, which they say is common in people my size. I feel good. Everyone says I look good, but I have to stay here with the doctors and nurses until I get better.

Mom and dad came this evening around 7:00 and I had a bandage on my leg which I hated and tried to get off, so I moved around too much. They are still giving me morphine and it seems to calm me down. I sure like to move. They say that I might have a rash, so they will put cream on me. I'm not doing so well now, but tomorrow is another day.

Day 4 - Saturday, November 24

I’m still kicking and feel okay. Mom and dad both came to visit today. I look so skinny but I feel pretty relaxed. The big news today is that they took the tubes out of my chest. It sure feels better now that they are out. I handled it okay. My belly button is pretty sore but they don’t seem to think it’s too bad yet.

After they took out the tubes, they left me alone to sleep. I really like it when they just leave me be. I don’t like everyone touching, poking and prodding me. I really like it when mom and dad come to visit. I like to hear them talk and when daddy calls me sweet thing. I think

I'll be okay today I've made it four days and I'm strong, so I'll be just fine.

PS. They also turned out the blue light. My jaundice seems to be a lot better and I'm looking healthier.

Day 5 - Sunday, November 25

I'm feeling good. I made it through the night just fine. Mom and Dad came to say hello and then went to see the nice lady social worker and had a talk. After they saw her, they came back to visit. I really wanted to open my eyes to see them, but I guess it's not quite time yet. Mommy stayed longer than dad, and we had a nice talk.

I seem to be stable, and there has been no bad news. They did physiotherapy on my chest so I that I don't get pneumonia. I handled that really well. My belly button is still very sore so they gave me medicine to fix it. Well, there is not too much else to say today, so, I'll just say see you tomorrow.

PS: Mommy brought me in some milk, but I can't drink it yet, so they put it in the freezer for later

Day 6 – Monday November 26

Wow, I'm still here. My heart rate has been up and down all day, but I feel pretty good. My belly button hurts, and they might take it out and stick a tube in my arm. OUCH!

Mommy came to see me. She was pretty sad. She cried and sang to me. I'm worried about her but I think she will be okay.

My nurse is really nice, but it's a good thing mom was here because when my nurse went for lunch my hand was caught under the respirator tubes and I couldn't move it. I got really mad and mommy called another nurse over to fix it so then I felt better. Thanks mom.

Day 7 – Tuesday November 27 – One week old

I had a pretty rough night last night. I kept having heart rate fluctuations, they call these braddies, so they are a bit worried. They also think I have an infection but don't know what kind, so they sent a lot of tests away to try to figure that out.

Mom and dad both came today but didn't stay too long. I can't wait until I can be with them all of the time. They told me last night that I have gained 20 grams. They are feeding me fats and things I need to get bigger. I hope that I get bigger soon. My jaundice came back, so they are doing phototherapy again. The doctor told mom and dad that the valve in my heart opened again, but they can't give me any more medicine until I'm more stable.

Mom and dad are so worried and cry almost every day. I think that I'll be okay and can't wait until this is over and they can take the tubes and needles out of me. I don't always feel so comfortable. Well, don't worry too much, mom and dad, I'll be okay. Everyone says I'm a fighter.

Day 8 – Wednesday November 28

Well, I made it past a week, and everyone is really pulling for me. I am still having braddies today but not as much. They took the IV out of my head to give it a rest and put one in my leg. I don't like it too much, but it's okay. They have a line in my arm to give me medicine and take blood. My belly is really big, and they took an x-ray to see if everything is okay. They think it is air because I've been having hiccups all day.

The nurse put a tube in my mouth to let the air out. I don't like it at all. Mommy and daddy came to visit when they put the tube in, and I made faces a lot. Mom and dad thought I looked cute, but how would you feel with a tube down your throat. I also had a braddy while they were here, and it scared them a bit, but the nurse fixed me up, so I felt better. I'm pretty stable, but who knows about tomorrow.

Day 9 - Thursday, November 29

Hello, it's me again. I'm feeling pretty good so far today. Mom came in the morning, and now she's gone for lunch. They are doing physiotherapy on me every four hours and suctioning my tubes every hour or so. Mom is so nice; she has been telling me stories all morning. I like to hear her voice.

I had a couple of braddies this morning, but it was not too bad. There is lots of gunk in my lungs and it makes me uncomfortable. I had a visitor today! Liz the nice nurse that I had last week. She came by to see how I was doing. She said I looked bigger do you think so? My belly went down a whole centimeter, so the tube in my mouth seems to be working. I hope that they take it out soon.

Day 10 - Friday, November 30

So, my jaundice is back again, and they have to put the lights back on. They took the line out of my arm, so all I have now is an IV in my head. They say that I'm stable, still having braddies but no one knows why. Mommy came to see me but didn't say much. I think that she was sad.

I gained 120 grams in the last three days, but they don't know if it is weight or just water and fluids. I now weigh 780 grams more than my birthweight! Mom and dad came back tonight to see me. I sure wasn't doing well. They only stayed awhile but I was so glad to see them. I think that I'm going to have a bad night tonight but if I make it through this one, I can make it through anything. I love you mom and dad.

Day 11 - Saturday, December 1

They did an ultrasound on my brain today and found that I was bleeding really badly; they call it a grade four bleed. They took off the phototherapy light again and I'm looking really tanned. Mom and Dad came in and said that they would make all the pain go away. I wish that they would. I'm having seizures that make my body shake. They call it abnormal movement. Mom and dad are going away for a day to Sechelt. I hope they try not to think of me too much. When mom and dad were here, I tried really hard to open my eyes, and they could see me open them.

Day 12 - Sunday, December 2

I'm still here but not doing well. Mom and dad didn't come today, which was too bad. There are so many strange people around. It is very bright out there, and I feel very sick. I wish that they would stop poking and touching me. I want them to take the tube out of my nose and let me be. I don't want to hurt anymore.

Day 13 - Monday, December 3

My eyes are wide open today. Today is also my last entry in this journal. Mom and dad and the doctors thought it best to let me go on to a better place. They took me to a lovely peaceful private room so mom and dad could spend some time with me alone. They took off the monitors and held me. I was so happy and content.

Auntie Christine came and held me and cried, she was sad. Grandma and grandpa and Uncle Jeff also came, and grandma held me, and everyone cried. Before everyone else came a nice Chaplain came and baptized me. He said a bunch of prayers while mom held me, and he put water on my head and said I would go to be with god. Mom and dad both cried.

After everyone left, the doctor came in and took out my IV and the tube from, my nose. Oh, that felt so good. I'm happy now. I just fell asleep I'm in my mom's and dad's arms. I love you mom and dad. Please always remember me.

A year or so later we planted a tree and spread some of Jaimie's ashes in her memory at Burnaby Lake Park. The tree is thriving and so tall and strong. This is one way we will always remember.

As we know, time heals all. It was a very hard time for Doug and me, but we persevered, we continued on with our relationship and two years later March 18, 1993, James Douglas Golding was born, healthy and happy and we could not have been happier. We were married that August 21, 1993 and are still married today. Like all relationships, ours has had ups and downs, but we raised our son to become a wonderful independent man of whom we could not be prouder.

Losing a child is the hardest loss. Our children are supposed to outlive us, and when they pass no matter what the age a part of your heart dies too and you feel that you can't go on without them.

This pain does heal over time, and everyone will heal at their own pace. Don't be afraid to reach out to family, friends or professionals, as no one can go through it alone, I was very lucky to have family support which helped Doug and I when we needed to talk or cry or even laugh. Then one day we seemed to be laughing more than crying and knew that life would go on.

When I was asked to write a chapter for this book, I knew I wanted it to be Jaimie's Diary. Now she will be remembered by everyone who reads this. My love for her is still strong and we will never forget.

Becky Golding

"When one door
of happiness closes,
another opens; but often
we look so long at the
closed door that we do not
see the one which has
been opened for us"

- Helen Keller -

10

IT CAN ONLY GET BETTER FROM HERE

"Sometimes it looks like poo, and sometimes it tastes like poo, but it's food, and you just have to eat it."
—My son, age 5

Deciding where to start is always one of the hardest parts of telling a story, especially one that has many facets. What do you focus on? Where do you go? What do you do? How do you do it? The only certainty is who the story has to start with, and, this time, it's me. The road that you travel, the choices that you make, the things that you think - these all come down to what you choose to believe. I am not a victim because I choose not to be. I choose to think of myself as a fine diamond, many-faceted, precious, and rare. I certainly have many less-than-great experiences to draw on. Sometimes, it seems like I've enjoyed the school of hard knocks just a little too much, but I have learned lessons along the way.

I was an immigrant to a new country who was beaten by the school-yard bully. It wasn't my fault; I just had a funny accent and was really little and, therefore, an easy target. I have experienced the hands of men from an incredibly young age. My ex-husband was a real piece of work, too, what with the things that he would say and the way that he made me feel. The losses that I have experienced, the deep, heartrending, life-changing losses - those are stories for another day. Now, I choose to tell the story of what the hardest hurdle for me was probably to overcome, a story of overcoming great odds and adversity and realizing my own inner strength in my battle against poverty.

This story is not all doom and gloom from the start. It starts when I was working full time in a roadhouse in a small town while my parents watched the kids. My shifts usually started at 7 p.m. and ended in the early morning hours. I worked six days a week for crap wages but great tips. I was getting to bed about 3 a.m. and getting the kids up at 6, then putting them to bed at 6:30 in the evening and heading to work. I wasn't getting much sleep, but it was working out really well.

Still, it was time for a change. My eldest was about to start school, and I thought that I should find a day job so that the kids would be at school while I worked. I needed to see them more than just once a week. So, I decided to move 500 miles away, far from everything that I knew and the help that was available, to find that day job. My eldest stayed with my parents since she did not want to move. It was a hard choice for her and my parents.

Looking back, I ask myself, what was I thinking? I left a stable environment to find that the place I had lined up to work had burned down two days before the move, but there was no turning back at that point. There was more craziness there, but that is a story for another day. So, I found a place to live and a full-time job, with training—but it was steady nights. My sister-in- law watched the kids at night but would drop them off at 9 a.m. I endured five days in a row with no sleep for eight straight months.

One day, I drifted off on the couch; I think it was mid-morning on the fourth day of one of these five-day stretches of sleeplessness. My 5-year-old was hungry, so she went to "cook." I awoke to find a complete disaster in the kitchen, with coffee grounds, oatmeal, and flour all over the place—at least I can laugh about it now. I realized that it was time to teach her to cook the basics in case I fell ill and could not look after them.

Since that job wasn't working out, I took another, at a global company in management. I was the District Administrator for Western Canada, which meant enormous responsibilities and a great deal of daily travel, but I loved it. However, two-and-a-half years and one hostile takeover later, I was out of a job again. My next one, at a temp agency, was not so great. It was a struggle to pay the bills. I was now a working single mom of two living in poverty - near destitution. My monthly income was $810, and my rent was $675, leaving me with just $135 for food, transportation, and everything else. That is not a lot to work with, trust me.

The struggle to make ends meet was all too real. Looking back, I can't say I was content. We had struggles and burdens to endure, and I was somehow managing to go deeper into debt, even though I was paying the bills and not falling into the payday-loan trap.

Nevertheless, I always tried to make the best of the situation, to see the bright side, to find happiness in everyday events. In reality, though, I was so broke, and broken, that even welfare wouldn't assist me even though I was a single mom with two kids barely making ends meet and going without the very necessities of life, a mom whose children accepted that new toys were a never-never thing.

Sometimes they would get a hand-me-down, or Nana and Papa would get them something when they went up for the summer to be cared for while I worked after school let out because I couldn't afford a sitter. Food was a non-existent essential item in our house, and the government, which was supposed to be there for us, said that I made too much to qualify for assistance. "I make too much?" I asked, "even though I would have made more sitting at home on welfare?" The meager $53 that I might have received monthly would have made a world of difference in our pathetic lives.

It is appalling to think that the government would rather keep you unemployed than give you a bit of help so that you can continue working and contributing to society and that you and your children mean so little.

Amid all these struggles, I met Alan. The last thing that I wanted to meet or have in my life was another damned man. After all that I had been through to get where I was - which, granted, was not that great a place - after all of the hurt, abuse, and emotional scars - which are more stories for another day - I was anything but interested in men. No man was going to come into my life and tell me how to raise my kids and then leave. Alan, though, was perfect: he didn't want to be a dad, and I didn't want him to act like one. There were no sad stories, just the here and now. I only saw him once a week.

I smoked back then. Cigarettes were $4.50 a pack, and coffee was free at work, so that's what I lived on. Two packs of smokes a week and free coffee. What a bonus if the kids left a forkful or two on their plates; that would be my dinner. Yay! Food!

One night, I was babysitting my niece, and all I had in the cupboard was a can of yellow pea soup, so that was the kids' dinner. I was tidying up in the kitchen when I heard my son say to his cousin, "I know, sometimes it looks like poo, and sometimes it tastes like poo, but it's food, and you just gotta eat it," Hearing that just about broke my heart. I must do better, I told myself; I have to try harder. The kids certainly deserved better than they were getting.

It also broke my heart when my daughter was seven and we were in Zellers - a retailer that sold dish soap, soup, or other necessities below cost to bring customers - and I saw her looking longingly at a doll but could only say, "I know, but not today; there's not enough money." It is terrible when a young child understands poverty and sadness so well at such a tender age.

So, I picked up a night job stocking shelves. The hours were horrendous, and the lack of sleep made me nauseous, but my kids deserved more. Since the second job was at night, I would put them to bed and have the upstairs neighbour keep an eye out for emergencies. That didn't last long, though; the schedule was too hard on my body, regularly until it was time to go home. Certainly not ideal, but you do what you have to do but I did get another job at the mall where the kids could hang out while I worked and check in.

Then, one day, Alan told me that he had heard of a job opening for an operator at a new monitoring station where the manager was someone I had worked with before, and I was well- trained as an operator. I always say you should leave a job on good terms without making any enemies because the toes that you step on today may be connected to the ass that you have to kiss tomorrow.

Since I had already worked directly with the new manager, there was no need to call for a reference. Also, I had obtained a written recommendation from the owner of the company when I left. I made the call and spoke to the manager; we reminisced about old times, and I was hired on the spot to start immediately.

This was great news; life was starting to look better. I was now making more at the new job than I had been at both of my old jobs combined. I was getting along a little better; the bills were getting paid; we were struggling a little less - but I was still broke. I wondered how I could be deeper in debt than I had been before. Part of the answer, it turns out, was family.

Family, you see, is especially important to me. We have always been tight knit; we stand together, do for each other, and are there for each other. Sometimes, this means helping with money or food. Members of my family looked after my kids sometimes (or had in the past), and I helped them out when I could because that is only fair. My son went over to my brothers on the weekends (it was his choice), but I was still being tapped for help. That is okay, though; it's family. They are looking after my boy, and I'm supposed to help.

A couple of years went by, and Alan and I were still seeing each other. He had started to spend time with the kids, and they liked each other. In fact, he and the children were looking for a more permanent relationship, but I wasn't there yet. He was even having them join his family for dinners and Christmas. I was starting to trust him more; he was worming his way in, slowly but surely making little holes in the wall that I had built around my heart, and it was starting to crumble. Slowly but surely, he was softening me up. He had become a constant in my life.

Anyway, Alan pointed out that I had been continually sending money to my family. Food to one place, money to another, helping with this bill or that. "You know, it's only February," he said, "and this year alone you have already sent over $600. You have to stop doing that."

I tried to justify it, and we had quite an argument. "How can helping out your own family be a bad thing?" I asked him. "Aren't you supposed to help your family?" "Well," he replied, "they all make more money than you do. Your brother's household has two incomes, and yours has one. Everyone that you are helping is taking advantage of you. I don't know why you can't see that. They all make double what you do or more, but they are still tapping you for money. You need to stop."

I sat down and thought about what he had said, and I just could not deny that he was right. This was not just an eye-opener; it was an epiphany! They were all taking from me. I was not getting as much in return. All of this "help" was to my detriment. The realization gave me a sinking feeling.

Less than a week later came the next phone call asking for funds, but this time I said no. I blamed Alan, saying that it was his fault, which, of course, was nonsense since nobody has ever made me do anything that I didn't want to do. A few days later came the next call, and I explained that I had sent such-and-such amount six weeks earlier and just could not afford it.

Then came another call: "Sorry," I said, "I just don't have it." The Bank of Fiona had closed.

It is amazing how many people stopped talking to me when the bank closed. It was a horrible, hurtful, and heavy realization that the only reason some members of my own family ever spoke to me was that they wanted something from me. That was a big, hard, nasty, harsh, jagged pill to swallow, and I choked on it. I was so angry. I was angry with Alan, who was the only one truly helping me. I was angry with all of those people taking and taking and taking. I was also angry at myself - in fact, I was mainly angry at myself because I had done this. I had created my own poverty. I had allowed myself to be used under the guise of helping. I had hurt my children as a result, and now I had to fix the situation. I resolved to find a better way of living.

I had to change my way of thinking. Alan was right. He was becoming my rock. Yes, I was helping others, but I was abusing myself. I was denying myself love. I was denying myself the ability to do things for myself because every spare penny that I had was going to someone who made more than I did, someone who chose to spend his or her money on unnecessary items. I should have been paying more attention to my own needs and wants. I began asking myself why it was my responsibility to dig them out every time. It was not an overnight change, but, eventually, the calls stopped coming. As a matter of fact, all communication stopped, and the silence was deafening. I felt lonely. Thank goodness for Alan; he called every night.

Soon, I was able to spend a little more on groceries, and that felt good. It was like an old Looney Tunes cartoon feeling. FOOOOOOD! I even bought a new microwave - not a big expensive one, but a new one. What a prize! Then we got a used computer and were able to afford internet service for school assignments. The sky was opening, and the sun was really shining! Then we took a trip to the zoo, where the kids found so much to see and learn. Life was indeed getting better. Debts were being paid; burdens were being lifted. It was all going well, one day at a time. I bought a new car and paid it off. I was able to save, and I'm saving still.

All of this improvement in my life came from accepting the fact that I had been hurting myself and realizing that I could not help anyone else until I helped myself and accepted that I am important too. That's right: I am important.

After my son grew older and chose to live with his father, Alan insisted that I move in with him, and life got better still. Moreover, our family all started speaking again. It took several years. The communication was halting and uncomfortable at first because, well, what do you say? I took my mum out to the mall one day, and she didn't say a word, even after I asked her to; there was just painful silence. However, this outing served as an icebreaker for both of us, as an awkward, moving, necessary first step. We are once again a unit, not quite as close as we were, but maybe that's the way it's supposed to be. I don't have all the answers.

Alan is now my husband. It took him years to wear me down by treating me right and convincing me that I am worth it, helping the kids, and fixing things that were broken (though it seems like it was me who needed the most repair). He helps me to cry when I need to and to laugh as much as possible, which is quite a bit. Throughout all of our trials and tribulations, he has stood by me and I by him.

We were married on the sixteenth anniversary of our first date. He managed to convince me that not all men are bad. He is my rock and my foundation, the first thing that I think of when I wake up and the last thing that I think of before I go to sleep. With him, I have learned to trust again.

Of the lessons that I have learned, the most important is that no matter what you are going through, you must never give up. The long hours are hard on the body, but they can help you to obtain the things that you need and strengthen your resolve to find something better.

Also important is the lesson that family is family: it's okay to help out when you can, but not to your own detriment, and it's okay to say no sometimes. Never give up because you never know who is going to enter your life and join you on your journey. Remember the Wizard of Oz: Dorothy started out alone, and then she met the scarecrow, and then the tin man, and then the cowardly lion, all of whom had goals of their own, and all of whom helped each other along the way.

Sometimes, life hands you what you need, and you just must accept the gift for what it is. Challenge your fears. The road to change is even harder than it looks and is harder than staying your current course. You may already need change, but you also must want it and be willing to work hard for it every day. There will be challenges and hurdles of all sorts along the way, but you just have to work through it, to go through it. So, stay strong, hold your head and shoulders back, put one foot in front of the other, and go through life one day at a time. There is a light at the end of the tunnel that gets bigger and clearer the more you work at it. You are worth so much, so NEVER GIVE UP.

Fiona Solly

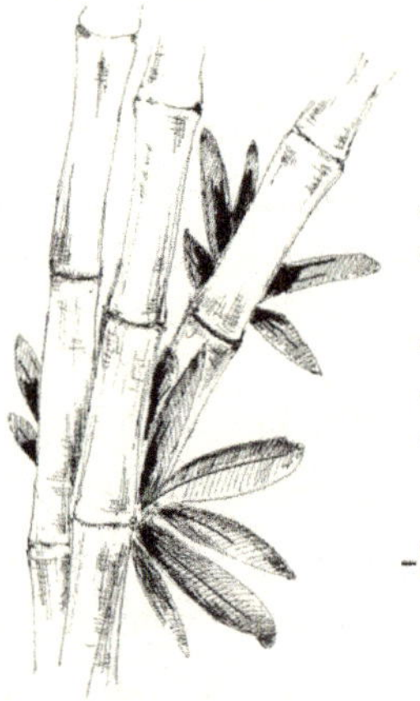

Eyes full of blackness
A hair on crimson drum
Is beckoning flight.

-Susan Harrison

11

THE JOURNEY BACK

THE MANY FACES OF MENTAL ILLNESS

This is my story.

"Hey, what's that sound?" My girlfriend and I were babysitting for my sister. I quickly checked on the baby; she was fast asleep.

The window was open, and we could hear some noise that seemed to be getting closer – louder. We could hear music and voices. We hung our heads out of the window and yelled "hey, boys, what're you up to?" One of the boys yelled back, "it's my birthday".

My girlfriend and I were super excited and thought, "should we invite them up?" Being the silly, teenage-boy-crazy girls that we were, we thought, "what the hell? – let's go for it". So, we called down to them and told them to come on up to unit 207.

Shortly afterward, we heard a knock at the door. In walked the most handsome guy that I'd ever seen. I think that it was teenage love at first sight. He said that his name was Allen; I told him that my name was September. Allen had an amazingly cute smile; it just melted my heart. He said that September was a beautiful name and asked whether it was my real name; I told him "yep, it's my real name". He responded, "love it!"

Allen put a case of beer that he had been carrying on the counter and offered some to me and my girlfriend. Allen had turned 18 years old that very same day – so he, like the rest of us, was under the legal drinking age. None of us cared, though; we were just having lots of fun, and Allen and I were falling for each other. We became an item overnight!

After Allen and I had been dating for a few weeks, I thought that it was time to bring him home to meet my parents. To my surprise, Allen and my dad really hit it off. They became super good friends – almost immediately. My dad even offered Allen a casual labor job. This involved lots of traveling as my dad was a long-distance truck driver. Dad and Allen seemed to have a great time together and enjoyed each other's company so much that my dad let him move into the room above our garage.

Whenever Dad was in town, our house became the party house. And, oh boy, were there parties. My dad and mom were both heavy drinkers. There was always a stocked bar at the house. Allen fell right into the party mode with my parents and soon, they were all hanging out at the local bar together. Given that I was 3 years younger than Allen, I wasn't allowed to tag along. Instead, I'd be left at home to babysit my younger siblings while my boyfriend was out partying with my parents.

Even though Allen and I had separate rooms in the house, we rarely slept apart. We were wild and free.

Allen eventually took me to meet his parents. His parents were quite the drinkers and, the day that I met them, his father was wasted, and his mom was drinking as well. Allen appeared to be very embarrassed; their home was unkept and there were empty alcohol bottles everywhere. After that initial visit, we rarely stopped by their home.

Allen and I moved out of my parents' place and into our first home when we were in our early twenties. We were so excited to have our very own place, and the parties continued. Given our backgrounds, having both grown up in homes where heavy drinking was a daily occurrence, we naturally continued down the same path.

Allen and I married in 1987 and, three months later, I was pregnant. Both of us eagerly awaited the birth of our first child.

Now that I was expecting, I stopped partying and started to take better care of myself. I'd like to say that Allen did too – but nope. He carried on just as before, hanging out at the pub and spending his non-working hours drinking.

Baby Ashley was now 6 months old. Allen and I decided to head out for a night on the town. I hadn't been out at all since Ashley's birth and Allen really wanted to take me out. So, I agreed, and we headed down to the local bar and stayed until closing.

When we got home, we were both intoxicated. We immediately passed out. It seemed like only minutes had gone by when I woke to the sound of baby Ashley crying; she wanted to be fed.

I got up and went to care for her, still tipsy. I was extremely nervous, even just picking her up, as I'd never been around her with alcohol in my system before. I was so mad at myself for being in this condition around our daughter. That night, I made the decision to stop drinking. One of us had to be sober – and I knew that it wouldn't be Allen.

Allen got a new job working as a mechanic on large semi-trucks. He loved his job and his coworkers. Allen would call me several times daily, just to say that he loved me and to check in on the babies; by this time, baby Claire had also joined our family.

Soon afterward, we bought our very first little house. We were all so happy. The girls had a yard to play in and Allen finally had his man cave.

After about a year, I noticed that Allen's calls to me during the day were becoming less and less frequent. Then, one day, they just stopped altogether. I also noticed that, during this time, when Allen came home from work, he would seem to be agitated and miserable. After dinner, he would sit in front of the TV with a beer, ignoring his family, and would then pass out.

Allen began to become verbally abusive toward me. He belittled me and called me nasty names. The abuse had started off infrequently and gradually but, eventually, it became a daily occurrence.

One day, I'd had enough. I sat down with him and told him that we needed to talk. During our conversation, it became clear to both of us that Allen needed to move out of our home. I told him that, if we were going to have a future together, he needed to get sober and to stay that way.

He moved into one of my sister's homes and stayed there for a year. Allen and I agreed that we needed to spend at least a year apart in order to wait and see whether our relationship was going to work out.

Allen surprised me and stopped drinking cold turkey. Our relationship started to improve and so did our communication. Allen and I were once again in love and he moved back into our family home.

Even though Allen was sober, his behavior did not really change that much. Over the years, he became increasingly distant and withdrawn. At times, it was like living with a sober drunk.

We spent most of our years together just going through the motions of a relationship. It wasn't until Allen started to have accidents at work, though, that I realized that something else was happening to him.

I knew that Allen needed to see a doctor – and for more than just the aches and pains that his job had caused. The weight and size of the equipment that he'd been using had been extremely hard on his body, and he had been experiencing serious physical issues as a result. But I'd also noticed that something just didn't seem to be right with him mentally.

We had a conversation about his mental health, and I told him that I was quite concerned about him and felt that he needed to see a doctor. To my surprise, Allen agreed with me.

The doctor diagnosed Allen as suffering from severe anxiety and depression together with osteoarthritis. He immediately started to take medication and, after about a week, Allen had become a different person. His personality became cheerful and light for the first time ever. I was seeing a new man.

When I look back on our journey together, knowing what I know now, the signs of Allen's illness were visible everywhere.

I could now understand why he had behaved in a certain way whenever he'd found himself having to be in a new and unfamiliar situation or environment. He'd become so agitated that he'd behave like a jerk. Family members would ask what was wrong with him and why I put up with his insults. Our daughters didn't want to spend time with him; he just wasn't nice to be around.

It made sense, now, that a lot of his drinking had stemmed from – and represented an effort to cover up – two things: the physical pain that he felt in his body as a result of the osteoarthritis and his anxiety. For so many years, he'd been unhappy but couldn't explain why. He'd just shut down and buried himself in the bottle.

All those years, he'd felt that people were picking on him and putting him down. He couldn't ever see that it was he himself who was causing the problems in his life. Now, Allen has developed an awareness of what's happening and why.

I'd encourage anyone who's living with a family member who you may have written off as being "a jerk" to take another long, hard look at that person. Think back over the years: could something else have been the cause of their behavior?

I've heard it said that drinking is a symptom of a problem – not necessarily the problem itself. In Allen's life, this was exactly what was happening with him.

Allen is now much happier, living a full life and enjoying our grandchildren. With the help of medication, he's become a different person. For that, I'll be eternally grateful. Never give up on the ones you love.

September

"Stop wearing your wishbone where your backbone should be."

- Elizabeth Gilbert -

12

DOING IT MY WAY, AGAIN

SURVIVING IN THE WORLD OF SMALL BUSINESS

The decision had been made – all I could do was try my best. And that's exactly what I did: my best. It wasn't always the wisest or best decision, but it was mine.

I left my security behind me and ventured out to "make it on my own".

Sechelt was definitely where I needed to be: my hometown, my comfort zone. My son had been born there. Some might say that Sechelt is a boring, little sleepy town where there is nothing to do. It's not a place for everyone.

Maybe that's why I like it here so much, though. Sechelt is a sleepy little town. It's located on the Sunshine Coast of British Columbia – about an hour outside of Vancouver, plus a 45-minute ferry ride. I really do live in a little piece of heaven.

What could I do to earn money? I'd chosen to quit school halfway through grade 11 – a real smart move! My dad said that I had to get a job or finish school. So, I got a job!

My first job was in a fish and chips joint. Then, I went on to work in many other factory-type jobs – plastics, cardboard boxes, glass bottles – as well as being a chambermaid (yuck!) and even having a stint at McDonald's. There were no real job opportunities on the Coast where I could use all of those mundane skills that I'd accumulated.

I did have a passion for creating, though. So – with no real training for any type of job in Sechelt – I put my thinking cap on. Could I possibly be self-employed? Why not? As I shopped and snooped around the local shops, I found there was nowhere I could get my beloved craft supplies. The lightbulb in my mind went on!

I hired some students to conduct a phone survey. It seemed that the Coast could use a craft supply store after all. Yeah!

I found a small space that was very affordable; it was pretty tiny and off the beaten path. I had shelves built, counters put in, and bought a cash register. I searched out suppliers and ordered paints, brushes, stencils, glues, pompoms, doll parts… you get the drift. Every day was like Christmas: opening boxes, discovering new purchases. Such fun! Pricing and displaying on the shelves. I'd found my passion.

I had a counter that was about 8 feet long. Underneath it, there were stools for the students who came to my classes. The stools were so uncomfortable, poor students!

I received a call one night from the police – someone had broken into the store.

Dang! Nothing appeared to be missing; products had been tossed about, and whoever had broken in had made a mess – but they didn't get what they wanted: cash. I left the till empty every night. Phew! Even had the Vancouver police come up and dust for fingerprints. The police had advised me that I should leave some change in the till so that anyone who might break in would feel that they'd got something and so wouldn't then trash the place.

Who knew? They didn't get anything – but it was nerve-wracking, to say the least.

Funny story: one time, I closed up the shop and headed home. I realized that I'd forgotten something, so I headed back to get it. As I approached my shop, I saw two distraught ladies peering out of the window at me. What the…?

Apparently, they'd gone to the back of the shop in order to use the washroom – but I'd forgotten that they were there, locked up, and headed home. They were pretty happy to see me when I returned! We all had a good laugh about it.

There might be a little lesson here: always have a final check before locking that door. Keys – check; purse – check; store bag of stuff that you take home every night – check; lights off – check; store void of customers – check.

As the business grew, the shop seemed to shrink. More people wanted to take classes than I had room to accommodate. I didn't want to run evening classes as I had a small boy at home. Ah – the balancing act.

I felt that I needed to secure a bigger space. Bigger is better, right?

I relocated to a 1200 square foot storefront on the main street. "Things can only go up from here", I thought. I added more inventory – who doesn't love shopping? – and created a bigger teaching area.

I brought in more teaching talent, and the classes boomed. We made lampshades, painted boxes, and created dolls, wind chimes, and jewelry. It was so much fun, everyone learning, laughing and sharing – for a while.

The crafting epidemic took hold. Tole painting became the "in" thing. So, paints were popular – and that's when the guys with the big bucks stepped in. Two of the local hardware stores decided that it was time for them to grab a piece of the pie. They brought in whole lines of the same paints that I carried. And, of course, the more that you buy in one order, the paint prices come down – so they could undercut my prices.

After that, Crafts Canada came along, followed a wee bit later by Michaels. Michaels killed Crafts Canada – so you can imagine what it did to my poor little shop on the Sunshine Coast. These megastores were in Vancouver rather than Sechelt itself – but that short 45-minute ferry ride makes for a nice day trip of some shopping and lunch.

I was doomed. Another plan had to be made.

In the meantime, beading had become popular; jewelry making was sweeping the Coast. I found a little hole-in-the-wall store of around 400 square feet; it wasn't easy to find. I knew that this little gem needed exposure – a huge sandwich board on the main street letting people know I was in the back – the shack in the back.

I crammed this little space full of shiny, pretty things: beads that glittered and sparkled, gleaming gemstones, and everything necessary to make these beauties into fabulous jewelry. I hung up tinkly wind chimes and had all kinds of fabulous gifts that made people smile. The "Knick Knack Shack" was born.

This was my happy place, glitter, sparkle, and shiny bits in every crevice of this quaint little shop. Going off to work every day was a good thing. In this little shack-in-the-back, I met people from all over the world – and the most wonderful local people as well. People reached out to me – people I will never forget.

One lady in particular offered to help me out by covering the shop so that I could take little breaks. She would just pop in and ask me if I needed to pop out for a bit. She has stayed with me all these years; she still pops into my store to see if I need a break. This little lady has become my "bestie" and we have shared a lot of life's little treasures, both good and bad – but we always come out on top. She is a friend for life.

Another woman offered to help me, with no expectation of wages or remuneration. She said that she just wanted to help. She stayed for a season. Can you believe that? – a friend for just a short time but one who will never be forgotten. She helped and moved on: an angel who stopped at my door. People come into your life for a reason, a season or a lifetime. We had some good times with my little Knick Knack Shack.

Bigger isn't always better – lesson learned.

I sold my little gem to a couple from Alberta. "I can do something else", I thought, so I sold the store and took some time for myself. It wasn't long before I was back to worrying about what the next adventure in my life would be. I knew that I needed an income. Geez: what could I do?

Running out of money and with no solid plan, I took a part-time job babysitting two adorable little munchkins. Who would have thought! We had lots of fun creating chaos. Even so… who wants to babysit for the rest of their days? The kids grow up and then they don't need you anymore; time to move on.

I landed a job at "Wine & Roses". Yes: we made wine from kits and made the most wonderful rose bouquets. Lots of male customers came in – wink – but buying flowers for their loved ones – sigh. But I did learn how to fashion a striking bouquet of flowers that many a man admired. It was a fun job, making people happy. Who doesn't love wine and roses? And making people happy!

The owner became a grandma and was ready to move on. I then became the proud owner of Wine & Roses: a perfect match. After a couple of years of backbreaking work, lifting 80-pound cartons of wine on and off shelves, the novelty of making wine wore off. So, I sold my beloved Wine & Roses to a strapping young man; he had lots of brawn for lifting.

This might have led one to believe that the grass is always greener… "Now what?", I sighed.

Another business opportunity opened its door to me – and it was perfect. Who wouldn't love to have a store that carries different, exciting products? – and a store that only required you to work a couple of days a week? A store where you had around 20 odd women – at various stages of menopause – working with you. Fun, right? Ha! I purchased Mosaic Market and it became my next challenge: more fun. It needed a facelift, some new blood, and more customers. Every year, Mosaic Market grew. Sales improved. Customers returned. Things were looking good – and kept getting better.

With Mosaic Market, I believe that I've found my calling. Mosaic Market is a slightly different retail concept. I rent space to vendors; they decorate their "space" and then fill it with their wares. The vendors are also required to work a certain number of days per month. This leaves me with just a few days a month on which I need to work in the store. It's a win-win situation. Everybody's happy – most of the time. I learned patience, this time, with Mosaic Market; you need to have a lot of patience.

We have a huge shark mascot who lives in a boat out the front. He's been named Sharkey. People began to take their pictures with Sharkey and so he has become a small-town novelty.

One day, I went to work – and Sharkey was gone! His disappearance was no easy feat as he had been secured to the boat. Who would do such a thing?

Details of Sharkey's disappearance were posted on social media. The newspaper even announced that he was missing. We thought that we'd never see him again. I was amazed at the feedback posted: kids missed Sharkey, the public wanted to see him returned; everyone was upset about it.

A few days later, I received a call: someone thought that they'd seen him on the beach in the next town. I drove down and scoured the beaches, thinking that the tipoff must have been a hoax. "Just one more corner", I prayed; "he must be found".

Low and behold, there lay Sharkey – in a ditch, just off the beaten path. He was a tad dirty, with a few bruises, but I knew that he'd survive the ordeal. He was secured to the boat twice as tightly on his return.

We held a "Welcome Home Sharkey" party – newspaper coverage and all. Only in a small town like Sechelt would you see people pulling together like this.

So, with patience – and some understanding – I learned that, if at first you don't succeed, try again: don't give up! You'll find your calling and be happy doing it; I did.

Through all my shenanigans, my son grew to be a very wise, thoughtful and handsome man. He and his wife are soon to become parents. And boy, is this gramma one proud peacock!

Kathy Trites

Green unfurling born
Shooting skyward uprising
Mounting an attack.

-Susan Harrison

13

BEYOND ABUSE

DO YOU EVER REALLY ESCAPE?

What does a 16 year old girl know about where her life will take her? She dreams of her wedding day; she dreams of romance; she dreams of graduation and of her life beyond, of a family and baby names and - STOP. That's all perfume and flowers and not how it went for me.

I can remember things back as early as maybe when I was 10 but really need something to jog earlier memories. My older siblings help out; they have told me about traveling in the summers when we went camping, Christmas, and the fun that we always had at the beach, with my mom teaching us how to swim and us riding on little cars and learning traffic signals. I am not sure, though, whether those are actual memories of mine or their suggestions; I could be associating photos that I have seen with memories.

In any case, those happy times and thoughts make me smile - times when my parents were happy (I think) and the laughter of me and my siblings was still in the air and we were still kids. I do remember my mom working lots of overtime to make our vacations and Christmases good ones and the year we all got bikes that she had purchased used and worked hard to paint and make all nice for

Christmas morning. I remember that it was always my mom who did things for us; it was she who arranged all the vacations, packed us all up, and made all the special holidays fun for us—never my dad; he was just along for the ride.

I played a lot of sports when I was around 10 to 12 years old. I loved track and field and was good at the events. I won medals at meets and was proud of my accomplishments. My mom used to take me to meets and cheer me on. Those days ended when I hit high school and all hell broke loose. I dropped out of sports and got in with the wrong crowd, and my schoolwork began to decline. I started to become a person whom I did not like because I was only trying to fit in. I became a bully, something that I hated, and when I looked in the mirror, that's what I saw. This sad tale begins when I was 13.

I was not so fortunate in my teenage years, but there were happy times with my friends through all of the crazy and silly things that we did. High school for me was not a place for learning, though; it was a place for rebellion and destruction. Here I was, 13 and already growing up so quickly. I missed that transition from pre-teen into a teen and went straight into being a rebellious young adult.

My home was unsupervised since my parents were constantly at work, and, even when they were home, they might as well not have been. Dysfunctional is a good way to describe my life; it was not like some of my schoolmates, going to dance practice or baseball or soccer. My life was mowing the lawn, doing chores, and drinking Potter's whiskey on Friday nights in the alley behind the house with the gang. With only 50 cents a week for an allowance, we would all pitch in and either buy booze or a hit of acid (the drug of choice back then), and someone would steal their mom's smokes, which made for a weekend you could just get lost in. "The paths we choose" without any adult guidance.

When my father fell ill that year, it seemed that the whole world came crashing down. My mother started to look for a way out; I guess all the years of raising kids on her own - since, again, my dad never really helped or supported her emotionally - took its toll. His illness made him like another child to care for, and she soon became lost in fantasies and dreams about how her life should be. Though I know that she loved us in her own way, she distanced herself from us kids, leaving us to our own devices, and, with no parental guidance, we depended on each other - and what do children know? What advice can they give each other? What experiences can they share at that age?

It felt as if I were looking through a window watching my two parents. One I could see ironing and staring into another world, disconnected from her real life, and reaching for something else; what that was, I don't know, except that it was not home life. The other I could see sitting in the living room engrossed in an old black-and-white TV, oblivious of everything going on around him, consumed by his illness, his survival mode having kicked in, and having no part in things. Where were the children running around and laughing and having fun being a family, doing family things? Where is that unconditional love from our parents?

A HUG, A WHISPER, A KISS UPON YOUR HEAD; MY WARM PLACE OF EMBRACE, YOUR UNCONDITIONAL LOVE. (Wren)

The path that I was going down became apparent very quickly. Fourteen came fast, and the drugs got better. MDA came on the scene; they called it the love drug! The name was pretty accurate, as I lost my virginity at an early age. Silly girl - I thought that I was in love with an older boy; he laid me down and promised me the world and left me there after a few minutes on what should have been one of the most important days of my life.

I was so ashamed and so hurt, and I ached. I could hear voices from the other side of the wall, and then the outside door closing. I lay there, so many things flying through my mind - what did I do? Why did you do that to me? I could feel the wetness between my legs and the ache in my belly; shifting my body, I sat up and swung my legs off the bed and then stood and, as I turned, could see the blood on the bed sheets. OMGGGG, someone is going to see that! Should I pull the sheet off? Panicked, I just pull my underwear and my jeans on and threw the sheet over the blood. My heart is racing, my mind reeling.

I pulled myself together and stared at the door for - a few minutes? I am not sure how long it really was; it was all such a blur. When I opened the door and came out of the room there was no one there. He had left with his friends. I remember hearing him laughing; was he laughing about me and what he had just done?

I stood there alone in horror and disgrace in the basement of some house for what seemed an eternity and then realized that I had to get myself home by myself. I had no money, and there were no cell phones back then; hitchhiking was my choice of transport that night.

Tormenting my mind as I stood out in the cold, rainy night hitch-hiking alone in the dark after a traumatic experience of consensual rape (if there is such a thing) was the question, where is my mom? I needed to feel her arms around me right then and to hear her tell me everything would be okay. Why didn't someone stop him? Here I am, my face wet with tears, trying to settle down, trying to make sense of it all as a car pulls up and the stranger within agrees to take me home - thank gawd for the rain washing away the tears that you now cannot see.

TIME DISAPPEARS SO QUICKLY LIKE TEARS IN THE RAIN! (line from a movie)

Fifteen: what a year of self-destruction! Sneaking out my bedroom window at midnight to go party and coming home just in time before my parents rose for work. I discovered a new drug, angel dust (whoa - that was some crazy shit) and also how to pleasure myself, not that the two go hand in hand (no pun intended), but discovering my own body was not only amazing but also led me down a misguided path of chasing that pleasure.

It was a year of being out of control, rebellious, angry, with an attitude! I was expelled from school several times, a badge that I wore proudly. I considered myself a badass and asked myself why I wasn't in a gang - how cool would that have been?

The day finally came when they kicked me out of school; I guess that they could only take so many stink bombs in the hallways, rotten apples squeezed into lockers, toilet paper fires in the washroom, cigarettes on the front steps of the school, and so on. Education? Of course, I never attended class! And now I was being kicked out? What are my mom and dad going to say? I am so scared (sarcastic laughter). I will be punished and grounded - right. I think that my mom has almost had enough of my crap, enough of the phone calls from school; enough was enough!

Home life became like this. Mom would be going to her usual place after dinner, leaving the house to "go to the library" again, which was her code for meeting up with some guy. Dad, meanwhile, would be picking his nose and scratching his balls in the recliner that he loved so much, as always oblivious to what was going on around him.

He wasn't interested in our teen lives and would just call out for a drink or a snack. He was ill, but he had two arms, two legs, and a pulse. I was always such a jerk to him in my teen years. I don't remember ever having any kind of bond with him or receiving any encouragement or support from him. We were just his kids; he had passed on his sperm, and the rest was left to my mom.

Never in my entire life did he tell me that he loved me; I never ever heard those words come from his mouth, ever. It was just his way. When I think back, it's hard to realize that my mindset was not that of a normal teen (what is a normal teen anyway?).

I could only see myself as a rebellious young girl as I was forced out of my teenage years — what did the other kids think? Did they have great family lives? Did they have love? I guess that I just did not care. I was dealt the hand, and I played it.

I did eventually receive an education from the bad kid school. My mom was relieved that I was accepted, and I went kicking and screaming. The public called it the holy grail of dysfunctional teens, but it was a good school for me. I pushed through and learned one-on-one from amazing teachers.

I remember coming back from a camping trip with the school and my mom, when she picked me up at the ferry, just looking at me and saying that she didn't recognize me because I looked like such an adult. I guess that was the day she really did see me for who I had become.

However, as much as I am thankful for the few years I spent at the school, it certainly was not the traditional way of teaching, and I never had a graduation. I really missed out on that, though it never really concerned me until years later, when I started to wonder, what if? what would I have worn? who would I have I danced with? - all of the things that another 16-year-old would have been thinking about and looking ahead to when she graduated.

But I want to talk about the new drugs in those colorful, oh-so-special times. There was snorting some good old cocaine and the delightful opium that sent you tripping into another realm. My weekends were loaded with hallucinogens and boys - well, boys who thought that they were men, so not boys-to-men but men-to-boys.

I was 15, glorious 15. I had a couple more sexual encounters. I figured that I was not a virgin anymore and, really, there had to be more to it than what that useless selfish jerk who stole my virginity showed me, so why not get back on that horse and take it for a few rides? I might learn some new tricks. Well, I got nothing out of it, no sexual satisfaction. I just went through the paces and boys at that age tend to be "minute men," so the whole save-a-horse-ride-acowboy experience was a failure, as I somehow knew that it would be since I had no emotion during the deed. I was just angry and lonely and reaching out blindly. I thought that having sex would cure that craving but it was just more damaging.

Then, freedom! There is happiness in this darkened grey cloud that dwells over my head. I have met a boy, and we have been dating for a bit now, and I really like him. He treats me like a princess and is handsome and tall and all the things a girl wants. I am feeling so lucky to have found someone like him. We have had several sexual experiences that were gentle and kind and loving, and I finally learned what it was all about. I was so happy, I smiled all the time and laughed. I thought that I would just burst with happiness. Can this be real? Pinch me, someone, please; I don't believe this is happening to me.

We spent so much time together, and I never wanted to leave his side. I wanted to feel that blanket of love and warmth all the time. I bathed in it, I drank it, I relished in it. After a few months, I started spending the night with him more and more, and my parents just let it happen, no questions asked. I remember having sort of a conversation with my mom, and she pretty much just shrugged her shoulders; I guess she figured that I would just do it anyway, and I never even spoke to my dad about it at all. I guess that meant one less kid at home.

Sixteen: it was my 16th birthday! Happy birthday to me, happy birthday to me - WHAT birthday? There was no cake, no family, no love, no nothing at all. I had given myself a present already by telling my mom that I was "outta here!" I could not go through the motions anymore, though of course I didn't know what that decision at that instant would cost me. I called my new love and told him to come get me, that I was packing my stuff up and coming to live with him. He welcomed me with open arms, and my face lit up like he was my angel.

As I was waiting for him to come and get me, my mom came down the stairs with a box in a bag; there was no birthday wrapping paper. “Open it,” she said, handing it to me. Inside was an alarm clock. “I thought you might need this, for you'll have to go and get a job now.” There was no emotion in her voice or her face, I did not know if she wanted me to stay as she never whispered a word. Happy 16th birthday to me! I kept that alarm clock for 20 years.

So, I moved in with my handsome saviour, into his little place, at sweet 16. I thought that we would be in love forever. I don't remember exactly when the nightmare started. I thought that I had found someone to love me but soon realized that I was in the hands of a sick and sadistic control freak. My life just fell into the burning depths of hell !

PUNCH FEAR IN THE FACE! OR SHOOT AN ARROW AT IT THAT'SGOOD TOO! (Reone Rajput)

What say thee, oh Romeo, oh Romeo? There was no Romeo in this part of my life, only the devil in disguise leading the lamb to slaughter. We moved around a lot, never staying anywhere longer than a few months. The first year, though, was wonderful. We loved music and concerts and each other's company and had lots of laughter. We smoked a lot of weed and never did hard drugs - well, with the exception of magic mushrooms. We would make tea on a Saturday night and watch Monty Python on TV and laugh and laugh. We would go camping with friends - his friends, they were not mine and never would be.

I was so excited when I got a job. I worked at a pet store, catching fish, and feeding the small animals and birds. I loved it until, one night during closing, the owner locked up and walked over to the counter and pulled out some cocaine and started snorting it right there on the counter.

Looking up at me, he asked, "Want a line?" "No, thank you, I don't do drugs," I replied, it was just little white lie. However, the next day, I was let go, a fitting dismissal for a druggie like me.

I am trying to recall how the abuse started but just can't bring to mind when I felt that first blow and my heart being ripped from my chest. I think that there were little things to start with, my boyfriend pushing me and abusing me verbally, like calling me a "useless bitch" when I made the same meal twice in a row?

I didn't know how to cook; I was 16; everything came out of a box. Then he was pulling my hair, telling me that I would never leave him but would be with him for the rest of my life, shutting me in the bedroom because he didn't want to see my face. This was all a part of his effort to control me, but I thought that I loved him, and I became fearful of him. The combination of love and fear is hard to describe; your heart is so full that it aches, but at the same time it is pounding with fear. There may have been people I could have turned to - but I was scared and in love. I had made this big deal about leaving home. I was this badass chick living with her boyfriend at 16. I couldn't talk to his friends, and I had distanced myself from my siblings and school buddies, I had left home and isolated myself, but I think that was all a part of the control that he had over me. In my mind, I had made my bed and would have to lay in it. The control was getting worse and starting to include sexual abuse - sometimes it would be so bad it made me sick to my stomach.

Our lovemaking ceased to be gentle and loving, though this was the very thing that sent me running into his arms. Instead, it became increasingly violent and aggressive. Often, he treated me so badly it became painful, and when I screamed for him to stop, he would slap my face and cover my mouth with his hand. The tears would soak my face, but he could not see them because he was blinded by a rage that came from some hidden place I never knew was there. I was raw inside and out.

What did I do? Why am I being treated like a dog? My heart was not just broken but shattered into a million pieces never to be put back together again. I started to become a bitter and resentful person. I didn't know how to escape and figured that he would just track me down if I did and hurt me more. There seemed to be no escape but only endurance. The walls began to be built brick by every hated brick.

BLACK AND BLUE! WHATTA DO WHEN YA LIVE IN A ZOO? (Wren)

Seventeen and battered: I wonder if they even had shelters for battered women back then. At 17, would I be considered a battered woman or just a messed-up teenager? Would they even believe me? There were no marks, no burns on my body to prove that the abuse had occurred, and, even if there were, I didn't see how I could prove that he was responsible. I could imagine the medical evaluation: "You poor thing! Just take these pills and everything will be alright." Whatever resources there were for people like me back then were not widely known, so it would not even have crossed my mind that there was help for me outside of my family.

Then I found myself pregnant, adding one more problem to my messed-up life. I panicked. I cannot have a baby! If I told him, he would hit me for being so stupid as to get pregnant - as if he had had no part in it. I didn't know what to do. I was very scared and felt so alone.

Sitting in the doctor's office the room was cold and empty of compassion with its all white walls and sterile equipment. I reached my hand out to touch that horrible piece of paper on the padded table and noticed the posters on the wall about pregnancy and adoption and turned to hear the soft muffle of people talking in the other room as I sat there all alone, my mind wondering, my heart racing. I am so scared but need to put on my best brave face, I wanted to scream "HELP ME!" at the top of my lungs, but once again fear silences my screams.

The doctor told me that, because of my age, I needed parental consent in order to terminate the pregnancy and gave me a handful of pamphlets to read. I was left alone to make a life changing decision and termination was the decision that I made at 17 years old. On a Saturday morning, I showed up on the porch of my family home. It was a gut-wrenching experience, but it had to be done.

I went inside to find my mom in the kitchen and looked at her with anguish in my eyes that she never even saw. I wanted so badly for her just to grab me and take me in her arms and hug me and hold me hard and tell me how much she loved me and missed me and that she would make everything alright and beg me to come home to her loving arms - sorry, wrong movie!

"Wren, what are you doing here?" was what she said. I figured that I might as well be blunt and get it over with as quickly as possible. "Mom, I'm pregnant, and the doctor said that you need to sign this consent form in order for me to have an abortion." I put the form on the table. She looked at me with - pity? disgust? What did I see in her face, even for a split second; was that the love for a child? Was she thinking that I was so rebellious that, if she tried to talk to me, I would just shut her down? I will never know what she felt that day.

She reached for a pen, scribbled her signature on the form, and said, "Oh, Wren, if this is what you want" there was no heartfelt conversation. Then she asked me if everything was okay, and I told her the biggest lie I could muster up. This could have been an opportunity to escape the hands of that monster, to turn my life around, but once more love and fear conquered me. "I am doing okay, mom," I lied. I left feeling so defeated and cried like a baby - I was a baby carrying a baby - I cried for a very long time.

Scared as I was to tell him that I was pregnant and had booked an appointment to have an abortion, I waited until the last minute to say anything. As expected, he told me how stupid I was for getting pregnant - what the hell was I doing? He did not want kids right now; but I knew that, so I knew that there would be no disagreement about terminating the pregnancy.

Doing so left me with bitterness and hatred and a slice of agony in my heart. I don't remember the day of the procedure or thinking about the loss of what could have been, torn from my life out of fear. I don't even remember who took me to the clinic. I want to think that it was my mom, but more than likely it was a sibling. I do know that I didn't go back to my home that day but to someone else's, and I remember the feeling of a warm hug for a few hours, but it is so foggy in my mind that, no matter how hard I try, I cannot see it clearly.

SADLY ENOUGH, THE MOST PAINFUL GOODBYES ARE THE ONES THAT ARE LEFT UNSAID AND NEVER EXPLAINED. (Jonathan Harnisch)

Isolation and degradation now filled my waking moments. He moved us to a house that we shared with roommates. They were fully aware of what was going on but all turned a blind eye, even when my eyes were swollen from tears. They discovered hard drugs, but I never partook, thank gawd, and he never forced me. I liked my drugs, but I was not sticking dirty needles in my arms. I wouldn't even watch when they shot up in the back room, but I certainly experienced the destructive aftermath: when he got high, things got real!

He threw me against the wall one night (well, many nights), and I fell behind the bed, and he proceeded to punch me; the pain went shooting through my head and my arms as I tried to protect myself. Then he put the boots to me, kicking my legs and bum, yelling horrible profanities at me, and "why did I get stuck with you?"

I was crying out for help, but no one came to my rescue. I curled up in the fetal position crying, "stop, please, just stop," and, eventually, he left me there battered and defeated. "Don't you dare come out or you'll get worse," he said as he left the room. He came to bed that night and sexually abused me. It wasn't making love or having casual sex anymore; it was this fiend ripping at my flesh and soul, I had so much my pain and hatred in my heart.

The next day, one of our roommates finally saw me, I mean really saw me, and said something to him. "Shut the hell up and mind your own business," my boyfriend told him. He moved out a week later.

I saw a dead person that year, a man who died from an overdose there in our house. I was horrified at first. I couldn't see much, as the room was so dark, and then they came and took him away, and I was left standing there staring blankly and, I realized, without emotion. My hardened heart did not feel pity or sadness. I wondered how I had become so distant from emotion and other people, and also how I had become so fearful of my boyfriend.

Why don't you just leave? I asked myself. How the hell did I get here? I might as well be dead like the guy under the sheet since no one cared, or that's what I thought, and I hadn't given anyone an opportunity to care. It was that combination of fear and love again. I was too scared to reach out to my siblings or mother or even an old friend. I began to wonder whether this psycho would kill me one day. When we soon moved again, it was to a place without roommates. I suppose he didn't want his friends to start saying bad things about the way he was treating me - out of sight out of mind.

We lived in a rundown house in an isolated industrial area where there were no grocery stores, shops, or places for me to go. The power that he exercised over me peaked at that time. He was coming home drunk more often now and waking me up at 2 am to sexually abuse me. His breath had an awful smell like alcohol and stale cigarettes, and I had to turn my head away as I could not let him kiss me. He would get angry and squeeze my teared soaked face till it hurt. I became an object for him to do with as he pleased.

Those nights never lasted long because he was so drunk; he would just roll off and fall asleep. I would quietly go to the washroom after he passed out and throw up and clean myself and just cry. Weeks seemed like months in that house. He left for work after threatening me not to leave. My existence was empty. I was just there staring at the walls, wishing my life were different, trying to make sense of how I got here.

Was I on a journey of emotional imprisonment leading to death? There was no TV, so music became an escape for me at that time (as it is to this day). The elaborate stereo system became my best friend, getting me through the lonely days and the abuse. I would dance in the house and play the music loud when he was gone and sing and dream of places I wanted to go and escape from this prison with no bars. It was a small piece of sanity until he came home.

Then it happened, he went too far. He came home late one night so drunk, I had fallen asleep on the couch and he woke me up by grabbing me by the hair and dragging me up the stairs where he threw me onto the bed. Then he jumped on top of me and held me down and choked me while fixing me with a demented stare. I couldn't breathe or scream but only kick my legs. PLEASE NO! I'm sorry, I'm sorry is all I could think in my panicked mind, whatever I did I'm sorry, please stop stop stop, and blackness overwhelmed me. Sometime later, I don't know how long, I opened my eyes again. My throat was aching, and I had a hard time breathing, HOLY CRAP! I thought that I had died. I turned to see him lying there passed out. I wondered if he even knew what he had done if he knew whether he had killed me.

I put my hands to my throat and my tears poured like a river. I moved quietly off the bed and went downstairs and sat in the dark for hours until it was almost time for him to go to work, telling myself over and over that I had to leave, to make a phone call and go; otherwise, I would be dead the next time. I snuck back upstairs and got back into bed just before he woke up. When he did, he didn't check on me or say a word. Whatever rage overcame him made him oblivious.

That morning, as I looked in the mirror at the bruises on my throat and eyes puffy from crying, I could hardly breathe, so overcome was I with emotion and realization of the whole ordeal. Finally, I grew some woman balls and made a phone call to one of my siblings.

They couldn't believe what I was telling them, emotions and tears distorted my voice as I told the story for the first time about the horrific life that he had been forcing me to live. "Just throw your clothes in garbage bags," they said, "I'm on my way."

I was panicking and hyperventilating with real fear as I waited on the porch with the three green garbage bags into which I had packed all of my things and crying because someone had listened and was coming. I was almost 19. When they pulled up, I wanted to scream with joy. My body was shaking, and tears of relief flowed. I hugged them like I was never going to let go. They cried with me, understanding now what I had gone through the past three years.

We had just left and were at the end of the street when he pulled up to the house from the other direction. I had done it; it had taken a near-death experience, but I had gotten the hell out of there. He did find out where I was staying and pursued me for some time until I called the cops, and he finally stopped.

MURDER'S OUT OF TUNE, AND SWEET REVENGE GROWS HARSH. (William Shakespeare)

The freedom that I pursued at age 16 became an unexpected nightmare. I paid for that freedom with rage, sadness, pain, and self-blame. That freedom left me unable to trust anyone. It created walls that remained for many years - until my best friend, my knight, chipped them away piece by piece.

At the time, I didn't see my escape from the monster as freedom but rather as the beginning of my future life. What would I do with it? There were not a lot of resources for teenagers back in the 70s as there are today and of course were no cell phones or personal computers.

I never sought help for the mental and physical damage that I suffered. In fact, I have never fully disclosed much of this period in my life until now. It was a very emotional and raw journey to write these words, and many times I had to stop because remembering and finding the words to bring my story to life brought me to tears. I have written a general account of my teenage years; there were many more incidents that would take an entire book or journal to detail. Maybe I will write about them one day, but just this much has been like a kick in the gut.

I hope that this account will convince parents to help their children, no matter what they have done, to escape from abusive relationships and to overcome addiction and other self-destructive behaviors. There is help and guidance out there. Just be sure to keep the lines of communication wide open.

Likewise, young people need to know that they can reach out to friends or family or call a hotline or walk into a clinic. Don't hesitate to use all of the resources at your fingertips. Don't wait, like I did, for the lights to go out!

Fortunately, my life turned out more or less alright. I have been married twice. The second marriage, to my knight, has lasted for 22 years now. I have never allowed anyone to abuse me again in any way. I have beautiful, smart, amazing, and successful children whom I am there for every second of every minute of every hour of every day. I will continue to guide them the best I know how and love them unconditionally for the rest of my days.

As for my family, my father eventually succumbed to his illness when I was in my early 20s. We never did develop a bond or relationship, though I was there when he passed and told him goodbye and that I loved him—but he never said those three little and most important words to me before he closed his eyes forever.

I reconnected with my siblings around this time. It was slow at first, but, in my later years, our relationships grew stronger, and I developed and have maintained a special bond with most of them.

I also reconnected with my mom in my early 20s. I never really experienced maternal love in my early years, but I felt something like it as our relationship strengthened over time. We have become good friends and laugh together again. I forgave her in my heart for not being there for me as I came to understand the pressure and loss of connection that she endured in those times. I could almost say she was a victim in her own reality.

She doesn't know about my struggles and the abuse that I suffered during my teen years, and I will never tell her. She is old, and her memory is not what it was, so to tell her now would be pointless; all that she needs to know is that I love her.

I have had many colorful adventures since the early years of my life that were full of love, lust, despair, and addiction, but those are stories for another time. Sorry to leave you hanging.

LIFE IS FILLED WITH UNANSWERED QUESTIONS, BUT IT'S THE COURAGE TO SEEK THOSE ANSWERS THAT CONTINUES TO GIVE MEANING TO LIFE. YOU CAN SPEND YOUR LIFE WALLOWING IN DESPAIR, WONDERING WHY YOU WERE THE ONE WHO WAS LED TOWARDS THE ROAD STREWN WITH PAIN, OR YOU CAN BE GRATEFUL THAT YOU ARE STRONG ENOUGH TO SURVIVE IT. (J. D. Stroube, Caged by Damnation)

Wren Beaushea

"Everything
is within your power,
and your power is
within you."

- Janice Tractman -

14

POSITIVITY MAKES ALL THE DIFFERENCE

YOU ARE ONLY HURTING YOURSELF

It was early in the brand-new year of 2018. While scrolling through posts on Facebook, I saw that one of my friends posted that she was going to be hosting a table at an all-day event called "Think and Grow Rich for Women". I had read the book *Think and Grow* by Napoleon Hill a few years earlier and was curious to know more about what this all-day event would entail.

I had always wanted to get to know Sara Williams better, too, and was excited at the prospect of sitting with her and her circle of female associates at her table. I wanted to meet new ladies and to expand my own friendship circle; this seemed like a great way in which to do so.

I swear, I must have been the very first person to book a ticket – and a seat at Sara's table. I sent her a private message through Facebook in order to let her know that I would be joining her. She responded to say that she was super happy to discover that I would be in her group for the day. During the lunch hour, Sara would be presenting a mini workshop at her table on how to run your own event. I thought that this sounded great; I had always wanted to learn a bit more about how to go about running an event of my own. So, I was all set and very much looking forward to it.

Over the course of the next month, I became increasingly excited in anticipation of the event. I already had a good group of friends – close friends – and enjoyed their company. But this event offered me the opportunity to do something completely different from my current career as a real estate agent. I felt pulled toward it; and I really wanted to expand my circle of friends.

For two years, I had been embarking on different courses and online programs on everything from public speaking to writing books to coaching. Having worked for over 25 years in real estate, I was starting to think about the next chapter of my life. I was extremely successful in my career; a team of agents worked with me and we were selling 65 to 90 homes every single year! I had been working pretty much 24/7 for several years and I was starting to feel burnt out. I wanted to take on a new challenge – something that I could be excited about, just as I had been in the early years of my real estate career. I also wanted to help others; I wanted to make a difference in other people's lives.

The workshop, "Think and Grow Rich for Women", was just what I felt I needed. And the thought of spending the day surrounded by Sara and other women who were moving in the direction that I, too, wanted to go in...well, I was like a kid waiting for Christmas morning.

I woke up on the day of the event – a snowy day in February – filled with energy and excitement. As I got ready for the event, I decided to ask my husband to drive me there because of the weather. As we reached the convention center, my excitement grew.

I went into the building, found the escalator. and made my way to the registration table. I looked around – but saw no one; I was the first to arrive. "No big deal", I thought, I'll have my pick of the seats at the table.

There were two lovely young ladies standing behind a table, getting things ready for the registration of the ticket holders. I approached them and gave them my name. I could see them searching though the list – but they were having trouble finding my name. I thought that I'd help them out: "I'm seated at Sara's table". One of the young ladies pulled up the list of attendees who would be sitting at Sara's table – but, no, my name was not there.

Finally, she said, "Oh, there you are; you're seated at Allyson's table". I told her that there must have been a mistake; I had registered to sit at Sara's table. With a smile, the young lady said, "Oh, Sara's table was so full that we had to move you to Allyson's table". I am sure that the expression on my face must have indicated that the worst possible thing that could ever happen had just happened! I responded, "Well, this wasn't what I signed up for". And, with that, I walked away to find this woman's – Allyson's – table.

The event room was full of tables and beautifully decorated. I was alone in the room and searched for the table that had been labeled with Allyson's name. Finally, I found it. As I was sussing out which seat was the best one, my eye caught the name on the table directly behind me; it was Sara's table. For a brief moment, I thought, "I should just go sit there, after all, I only came because I wanted to sit at Sara's table". But, in the end, I decided "no – then someone else would just be disappointed and that wouldn't be fair". So, I sat down at Allyson's table, feeling pissed off and extremely grumpy: the opposite of how I had felt when I'd arrived.

At this point, other women had started to arrive, and Sara's table was, of course, filling up. I could hear them laughing and greeting one another. Glancing over, I saw them all hugging; oh, they all looked so happy and excited to be together. Seeing that just made me feel even sadder about the fact that I was not with them. I kept my head down as other ladies arrived at my table. I didn't introduce myself and I'm sure that I must have been emitting some kind of ugly energy. No one even tried to talk to me – not that I blame them. I was acting like a spoiled brat.

As my table became full, and the room was filling up, I finally told myself "Don't be an idiot. Get it together or you might as well leave". I didn't want to leave, so, I pulled up my big girl panties and changed my attitude. I'm normally – and naturally – an extremely positive person. People have described me as being "inspiring" and "motivational" – but I doubt that, at that particular moment, the ladies at my table would have described me as being anything other than a 'grumpy bitch".

With the table nearly full, our table host, Allyson Roberts, arrived and sat down. She seemed warm, kind, and open; I was drawn to her immediately. She took the time to introduce herself to each of us – and I knew, right away, that there was something about her that I really liked. Now feeling much better, the event got underway.

At one point in the event that morning, Allyson was called to the stage. "Wow", I thought; our host was going to speak. She talked about her life and how she had ended up here, with us, today. She spoke of her struggles, her family, and her success. Allyson was a great speaker and, as I listened to her, I became more and more impressed with how she spoke and what she had to say.

During the lunch break, Allyson gave each lady at the table an opportunity to ask her a question. Allyson was intuitive in her responses. Now, I was even more impressed.

In the end, many other ladies tried to secure a spot at our table. We definitely had more ladies than we had chairs. Allyson did a wonderful job of going around the table and answering each lady's question. Some ladies were in tears – not tears of sadness but tears of happiness and reassurance in response to what they were hearing.

Then Allyson turned to me; it was my turn to ask a question. So, I decided to just go for it and to ask her if I was on the right track with my goals and dreams. Allyson said such beautiful and kind things to me that I, too, broke down in tears. They were not tears of sadness; they were tears of relief: I was on the right track in my life.

Funnily enough, I had completely forgotten about Sara and her circle of ladies who were right behind me. At Allyson's table, I found – and forged – a connection with the ladies there, and with Allyson herself. It was deeply moving and very emotional.

By the end of the event, I knew that I'd been put at that table for a reason. I accepted it; I embraced it.

A few months after the event, I pulled out my book, *Think and Grow Rich for Women*. Inside it, I found a card that I'd completely forgotten about; Allyson had given it to me. It was an offer to have a coaching session with her. I decided to take her up on it. So, I reached out to her through her website and booked my free call.

Well, the rest, as they say, is history.

Allyson helped me with a book that I was writing, she helped me to get my website together, she helped me with a TED Talk application, she helped me with a speech that I needed to deliver to a group of 160 ladies - and she helped me with so much more besides. I also supported Allyson; I even helped her with an event that she was running in my area.

I met a few ladies at Allyson's table that I become friends with – good friends. They're ladies whom I'll always think of fondly.

My life is now vastly different from how it was back then – when I was pulled from Sara's table and plonked on Allyson's table. My life has taken an amazing turn. I have written many books, coached ladies in sales who are struggling – as well as real estate agents – and I have become a certified numerologist, helping women transition to the next phases of their lives. I have spoken publicly about the importance of having a positive mindset and, as well, own publishing company, "Rock Star Publishing".

All of this came about because I did not sit at Sara's table. Well – *maybe* it still could have happened if I'd sat there but, deep down, I don't think so. I believe that some things are simply meant to be. I was meant to go to that event – and I was also meant to sit at Allyson's table.

What I want you to understand, for your sake, is the importance of "going with the flow". You cannot know why a particular door was closed or why a specific person left – or came into – your life. You cannot know why your job changed – or your relationship. We all have a path; we are all *on* our paths. The universe may say to you, "No, don't sit there, sit here". And if that happens to you – as it did to me – just smile and wait to find out why. "Why did it happen?" Well: there is always a reason – and it is almost always one that's in our best interests.

Julie Fairhurst

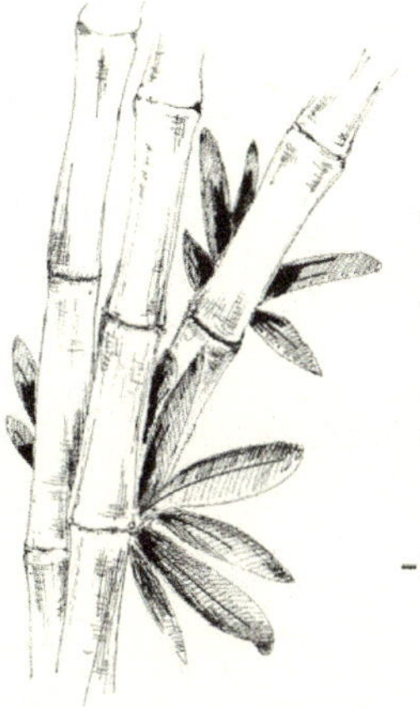

Twinkle twinkle blue
Uniting dots in heaven
Dream repressed anew.

-Susan Harrison

15

AUTHORS

Who are the women who have told their stories in Women Like Me. They are quite simply, women just like you.

Samantha Syvret

I am a mother of three amazing kids. I love my career as a hair stylist which I have been doing for 18 years now. I would not change anything that has happened in my life, which has been a whirlwind. I have been through many tough times, always looking for a stable home. I have lived in so many places in my life. I now live on beautiful Vancouver Island, in a home of my own and we are loving every minute of it.

If you would like to find out more about how you might be able to get into a home of your own, to help you and your family, here is the website to Habit for Humanity, for Canada and the United States.

https://habitat.ca

https://www.habitat.org

. . .

Christine Luciani

I am a young-at-heart 63 year old, mother of three fantastic children, nana to two awesome grandchildren, aunt, and sister to many, whether related by blood or not. I am also mom to three fur babies: My dog Harley, and two cats, Oscar and Pokey Joe. I was a stay at home mom until my children got older and then started working as a real estate agents assistant. I now work from home as a "virtual" assistant with my main focus on social media posting and marketing. I look forward to whatever is waiting for me next in my life. My newest goal: Driving to the east coast of Canada, I have seen the west, time for the east. Peace.

Michelle Bisgrove

I started as just Michelle, her own story, and soon to be a mom at 20 years of age. I had many last names, and each one defined me differently. As I had more and more children, that defined me as well. I am me first, or should I say, I have struggled to be so. I have had a beautiful and very full life with so many blessings. I am a mom of 6 children, a grandma of 2 so far. Diversity has been the road I have traveled; ran many marathons if you will. Anything from sky diving to bungee jumping with my kids. I have had so many adventures including traveling to amazing places in the world, I can't possibly begin to remember them all.

I have held my grandson through chemo, lived through drug addiction in my family, danced in the rain. Loved my heart out as much as I possibly can.

Always remember that this time next year, it will look different: wake up... get up and make as many people as you are blessed to love happy if you can. It's not about how many times you fall. It's about how many times you get up and make it good. I like to think I try and do that most days! I am very fortunate that I was born with a glass full kind of way. I think it makes a difference; genetics plays such a huge part of who we are!

My story is for anyone who might deal with not feeling worthy. Maybe someone who looks back and sees the dread of the past: past is forgotten, life should not be influenced by our emotions. It should be influenced by our actions. I am not qualified to be anyone's judge, not even my own. Live your life the best as you can and know that you can carry yourself wherever you need to be! Be vulnerable as much as you can every day. Listen, always listen. Sometimes you make choices in life and sometimes they make you.

Heather Scott

I am a proud mother of a son, a daughter, and a daughter from another mother (S.S.) They have blessed me with my 10 wonderful nana-children, ages ranging from 2 – 19, say what? A mother of a potbelly pig named Hunter who is now living a pig's life as a free-range pig on a forever foster farm with his free-range chickens. I've been blessed to have my younger sister and 83 year old mother (with dementia) living with me. I have a full-time career as a licensed insurance broker, and I'm known for going above and beyond for my staff and clients. I am so fortunate to have some of my loyal clients who have followed me for 36 years and who describe me as knowledgeable, compassionate, dedicated, effective and observant. I train newly licensed brokers to be the best they can be, sharing my experiences in a field, that is forever changing.

Sharon Jones

Live life to the fullest like it's your last day, never takes things personally and forge ahead. I have struggled and won and struggle and lost but always learned that is what we are here for … life's lessons and stirring the pot along the way.

I was born strong in 1960 and have 2 fabulous daughters who I would give the world to, they are beautiful and successful and strong independent women. My husband and I moved from the madness of the city just outside of Vancouver, BC to the much quieter, easy life on Vancouver Island in beautiful British Columbia with our 2 cats, Marley and Sophie where we love the peace and quiet of the deer, frogs, birds, crickets, eagles, hawks and all of the other nature noises. Wouldn't trade a thing, except the lottery would be nice.

Shelley Hatt

I live in British Columbia, Canada with my husband and fur babies. I love crafting and making gifts for others. I have a job that I truly enjoy working in customer service. I spend a lot of time outside walking and biking. Going on bike rides with my sister is fun and we try to do it as often as we can. I find peace in the outdoors. My granddaughter brings me so much joy. But my most favorite thing to do is to spend time with my husband.

Susan Daborn

What if I'd given up?

Writing my story was difficult for me, but eye opening. I have overcome so much in my life, what if I had given up? I would have missed all this beautifulness in my life. I'm so immensely proud of my daughter who has achieved so much for herself in such a short time on this earth. What if I had given up? How would life have turned out for her?

I love my little home in Nova Scotia where I foster dogs. I enjoy gardening and growing my own vegetables. I have close friends who mean a lot to me.

I am most proud of my determination and my business called Sue's Helping Hands (you can find me on Facebook) where I care for those with Alzheimer's in their homes. Not only do I help the patients, but I also help their families by relieving the burden from their shoulders, knowing that their loved one is well looked after.

I guess really, we can never know the outcomes for any of us, but I sure am glad I never did give up, look what I would have missed out on.

Facebook:https://www.facebook.com/Sues-Helping-Hands-852739001724552

Theresa Waugh

I was born in Vancouver, BC and put up for adoption at a very young age. Some of my siblings I knew, some of my siblings I didn't know till later in life. I was involved in a lot of sports activities growing up including professional springboard diving, which was my favorite. All that changed in a blink of an eye. I ended up getting married at 17 years of age and was blessed with seven beautiful children who are my life. I worked as a hairdresser for 18 years until I decide to go back to school and become an instructor. This career change was what I needed and with my children's support and understating I am able to really enjoy my work and career.

Becky Golding

I grew up in Prince George, BC and moved to the lower mainland when I was 18 years old. Shortly after moving I met my husband Doug. We were married in 1993 and are still happily married today. We have a son James who is now living on his own in New Westminster, BC. We have a rambunctious dog Riley and a cat Fruffles who both seem to rule our lives. We've been living in the same house for the past 18 years and are in a good place in our lives. I love long walks with Riley and hanging out in my yarden (yard/garden). I'm not sure what our future holds, but I'm open and up for whatever life throws at me.

Fiona Solly

Writing about yourself is always difficult. Deciding how open or how much you want people inside your soul is problematic.

How would I describe me if I were in someone else's shoes? I am hardworking. Whatever I set my mind to, I do. I have had setbacks and challenges all along the way but I have always maintained a sunny outlook and when I say I have taken time to stop and smell the roses, I mean that literally.

Helping people is in my nature. It's truly a part of who I am. Need a cake for a special occasion, I do that (as a hobby) and some of my cakes have been amazing! Dollicakes Creations on Facebook.

Guidance and being that bring light for someone, helping someone see a different way to brighter solutions, that's me too. Life Goals with Fiona on Facebook.

My children are grown with children of their own now. My grand-children are certainly a ray of sunshine in my life and my husband and I spend as much time with them as we can; sleepovers and baking together, going for outings.

Life is good, not perfect, but good.

Facebook
https://www.facebook.com/LifeGoalswithFiona
Facebook
https://www.facebook.com/DollicakesCreations
Email
f_solly@hotmail.com

September

My life has turned out so wonderfully, better than I could have imagined. My husband, who I love so much is doing much better now that he has discovered his illness and is getting professional medical help for it. My two daughters have grown into lovely young ladies. I have three amazing, sweet grandchildren, I just adore them. A few years back I was hired on at my local school board and it's a job I really treasure. I've made many wonderful friends there and look forward to the days I spend in my place of work.

Writing my story brought to light all the great things in my life that I can be thankful for. Sometimes when you are going through hard times, it's tough to see the good, but it's there. The good is always there, we just need to open our eyes wide enough to see it.

Kathy Trites

I was born in Vancouver, British Columbia and raised on the beautiful Sunshine Coast. After many exciting challenges and adventures off Coast, I decided to return home.

I have found my niche in the warm and encompassing enclave of Sechelt. It is here where my business thrives, and me and my very best fur friend Kiko spend our days, walking the beaches and exploring the woodland trails.

My biggest blessing in life thus far is coming in March 2021, my first grandchild. It is then that I will be able to put my creative endeavours to very good use and become the best grandma ever!

I would love for you to reach out to me through Facebook at Mosaic Emporium. You can also follow me on Instagram at Mosaic Emporium Davis Bay.

And, if you are ever visiting beautiful Davis Bay, be sure to drop in for a visit at Mosaic Emporium and say hi, I would love to meet you.

Facebook
https://www.facebook.com/mosaicemporium
Instagram
https://www.instagram.com/
mosaicemporiumdavisbay
Visit us at
4780 Sunshine Coast Hwy, Sechelt, BC V0N 3A2

Wren Beaushea

Well, I am not too young but not old either. I have advised the universe not to add any more years to my life (I laugh). I have had a most colorful life that I could not even begin to tell you as it was truly a very crazy and wild time in my earlier years! It was not till my late 30's did I begin to even remotely settle down but when I finally did it was most gratifying as the double life I was living melted away and all those massive walls that I had built stared to come down brick by brick.

I would have to thank my husband for that and for helping to ground me and for being my rock. I have an amazing husband of 22 years and 4 amazing children that were brought together as a blended family. Now try wearing those pants as they did not always fit! But we are very proud of all 4 of them and of ourselves for making it through those years (laughing) as it was a feat in itself to say we did.

We are now empty nesters, well almost empty nesters as we have replaced all the children with dogs, now we have gone from family to pack! We love to travel and do so every time we get a chance to. We have travelled all over Europe and Canada and the US, but have many places still not checked off our bucket list. We travel in an RV now and yes we take all the fur children with us when we travel, there are crazy fun adventures with the pack.

My hubby and I are planning the next chapter and adventure in our lives of owning a few acres far from the city and are looking forward to the country life and having lots of room to roam. I see a porch with us sitting on it drinking our morning coffee staring out onto the lake and listening to the early morning loons. I might even sit down and write about that colorful life of mine!

Susan Harrison

I am aged 64, mother of two and grandmother to one. I discovered at an early age that I liked to work with my hands and soon found myself pursuing a career in the trades. Now retired, I spend a lot of time in the kitchen, love to pair wine with food, and write haikus. I've also have a new found interest in natural and organic bath products, which I'm hoping to turn into a small home based business.

"If there's a book that
you want to read, but
it hasn't been written
yet, then you must
write it."

- Toni Morrison -

16

MEET JULIE FAIRHURST

I grew up in an extremely negative home environment. Alcoholism, emotional abuse, spousal violence, and poverty was rampant in my home as a child. It was a chaotic, stressful, and unstable place to grow up. If you have ever seen the television show called Shameless... well, that is exactly what I and my siblings grew up in.

I knew from the time I was a young child that I did not want to live this way. I do not know where it came from, but somewhere inside I knew it was wrong and I wanted to do better. But how? How do you do better when you were never taught a different way.

Pregnant at 14 years of age, married at 17 and divorced at 29, a single mother with 3 young children, with a grade 8 education, I thought my life was set to failure, following down the path of my parents. I was headed in the wrong direction.

But, somewhere deep inside, that young girl showed up and reminded me that I wanted better for my life. It wasn't easy, I had no support, from anyone, not a soul. I had to do it all on my own.

Was it an easy road, no it was far from easy. I was a single mom for 24 years. We lived off government handouts and I stood in line at food banks to feed my kids. At Christmas, we received Christmas hampers and I would go to the toy bank to get presents for the kids. The path we were on was not an easy one to change, especially when it is all that you know.

But I did it. I went back to school and finished my education. I built an outstanding sales career and won the companies top awards as well as being the first woman in the company to achieve top salesperson, year after year. I was able to buy a home, on my own and provide a stable environment to raise my children in.

Some people would say they never looked back, but I do, every day. Why? Because I never want to forget the journey that led me to where I am today. And today, my life is completely different. I didn't just fall into this new life, I worked at it, every day, all the time.

I now help others who are struggling in their lives. They may be living in poverty. They may have a negative view of themselves and an unhealthy mindset. They may be struggling in their career and feel lost. Just like I did.

If you would like to reach out to me for any reason, I would love to connect with you. Here is how you can find me.

Wishing for you, to be able to live your best life, the life you came here to live.

You can find me at:

www.rockstarstrategies.com

www.juliefairhurst.com

Follow me on social media:

Facebook: Rock Star Strategies

https://www.facebook.com/juliefairhurstcoaching

Instagram: Inspire by Julie

https://www.instagram.com/inspirebyjulie

LinkedIn

https://www.linkedin.com/in/rockstarstrategies/

Looking for Julie's books or free resources? Look here:

- Free Resources: https://rockstarstrategies.com/resources/
- Numerology: https://rockstarstrategies.com/work-with-me/#numerology
- Julie's Books on Amazon: https://www.amazon.ca/s?k=julie+fairhurst&ref=nb_sb_noss
- Follow my blog:
- https://rockstarstrategies.com/blog/

"You can have unbelievable intelligence, you can have connections, you can have opportunities fall out of the sky. But in the end, hard work is the true, enduring characteristic of successful people."

- Marsha Evans -

ACKNOWLEDGMENTS

Thank you!

I want to thank you for reading Women Like Me. It was an extraordinary experience for me and the rest of the women in this book. It can be hard dealing with past issues, bringing up emotions that have been held down for so many years. Everyone expressed a feeling of freedom being able to tell their stories to you. Some had tears, some did not think they could do it, but digging down, every one of them got their stories out for all women to learn from. I am immensely proud of each one of them.

Several people were instrumental in the production of Women Like Us

Amazon Bestselling Author and Self-Publishing Coach, Jennifer Sparks. – Jen is someone you want in your corner if you want to write a book or learn how to be self-published. Her knowledge is outstanding in the publishing arena. Jen was always there for any questions I had and was a guide for me to get this book published. I am incredibly grateful to have been able to work with Jen and look forward to working with her on more publishing projects.

Marc D. Baldwin, PhD Founder, Edit911 was a life saver in getting all the edits needed for the ladies in Women Like Me. For many of the women whose stories are in Women Like Me, this was their first time writing for a published book. Marc and Katherine (from his team) were gentle and had such kind things to say about each story. The little notes they gave to every woman was very encouraging and helped the ladies realize, they could do this.

Special thank you to Christine Luciani who was there along with me every step of the way. Christine, with her quick typing abilities and keen "eagle eye" was super helpful to me. Whenever I needed her she rose to the occasion and worked well into the evenings preparing the ladies stories for publishing. Without her, this book would have taken much longer and I am truly grateful to have her as part of my team.

And most importantly, to my husband Rob Breaks, who I love like crazy. He always believes in me and supports me in whatever I decide to do. Even when my ideas seem a bit wacky. Constantly by my side, encouraging me, listening to me and when needed crying with me. I am blessed to have him in my life. I sometimes wonder what I did to deserve such a great guy but then I quickly remind myself, that I am amazing too and he has me. We are both lucky people.